BEST OF
THE BEST

D0916531

D. ARTHUR DELAFIELD

Pacific Press Publishing Association
Boise, Idaho
Oshawa, Ontario, Canada

Edited by Glen Robinson
Designed by Tim Larson
Cover photos by Image Bank ©, Betty Blue
Typeset in 11/13 Century Schoolbook

The author assumes full responsibility for the accuracy of all facts and quotations cited in this book.

Library of Congress Cataloging-in-Publication Data

Delafield, D. A., 1913-
    Best of the best : twelve great Bible chapters / D. Arthur
    Delafield.
        p.   cm.
    Includes bibliographical references.
    ISBN 0-8163-1229-X
    1. Bible—Study and teaching. 2. Seventh-day
Adventists—Doctrines. 3. Adventists—Doctrines. I. Title.
BS600.2.D37   1994
220.6—dc20   94-3928
                                                         CIP

94 95 96 97 98 • 5 4 3 2 1

Contents

Introduction

The word *Bible* is a transliteration through the Latin and Old French of the Greek word *biblia*, which means literally "little books." There are many "little books" that make up the Bible. Honored and revered by most people, Holy Scripture is still read infrequently.

Consider thirty-nine books in the Old Testament, twenty-seven in the New Testament. The Bible canon equals sixty-six books, comprising 1,189 chapters, or 41,173 verses. The compilation of the Bible into books represents prolonged and diligent inquiry and research by Hebrew and Christian scholars. Separating the sixty-six books into individual chapters and verses is attributed to Stephen Langton, archbishop of Canterbury, in the late twelfth century. In the late thirteenth century, Cardinal Hugo divided the Old Testament into chapters as they stand in modern translation. In 1551, Robert Stephens divided the New Testament into verses as they are now.

According to the *Seventh-day Adventist Bible Dictionary*, pages 187, 188:

> The church did not create the canon or confer canonicity upon its books. The initiative in the production and collection of the sacred books rested with God. The church could only recognize and receive in faith the documents produced by divine inspiration. The development of the canon was a gradual process, presided over by the Spirit of God. . . . The hand of God led in the formation of the canon. The early Christians accepted as reliable only those books written by an apostle or a companion of an apostle. To be recognized as canonical a document had to have a wide acceptance among Christians throughout the Mediterranean world. They judged a work on the basis of con-

tent, its inner consistency, its harmony with the rest of Scripture, and its general harmony with Christian experience.

Ellen White testified:

God committed the preparation of His divinely inspired Word to finite man. This Word, arranged into books, the Old and New Testaments, is the guidebook to the inhabitants of a fallen world, bequeathed to them that, by studying and obeying the directions, not one soul would lose its way to heaven. . . . Men should let God take care of His own Book, His living oracles, *as He has done for ages* (*Selected Messages*, 1:16, 17, emphasis added).

Now try to imagine the difficulty of selecting from this treasure chest of divine inspiration twelve choice chapters and providing helpful commentary on the inspired verses.

These popular chapters correspond with the twelve senior Sabbath School lessons to be studied by Seventh-day Adventists around the world during the first quarter of 1995.

The selection was purely a matter of personal preference. Another author might have chosen different chapters. Several Bible chapters included those especially appealing to Adventists, for example, Revelation 14, Matthew 24, and Hebrews 11. Other chapters represent truths held in great reverence by all Christians, for example, Psalm 91, Isaiah 53, Matthew 5.

Best of the Best can be used as a supplemental reading resource for Sabbath School teachers. Pastors who love to base their messages upon strong biblical segments might choose to use these chapters as a basis for a series of Sabbath sermons.

The author hopes and prays that this book and its twelve messages will translate into the flesh-and-blood experience of many readers and encourage a change in heart and perhaps a change in lifestyle. Scripture has the power to transform as well as enlighten.

Chapter 1:

1 Corinthians 13

THE GREATEST OF THESE IS LOVE

Let me offer you something tangible: a free leather-bound copy of the Holy Scriptures in the version of your choice if you can even come close to showing me something, anything, any *thing*, in all the wide world greater than the love of God offered to us (see John 3:16) and made personal in His Son Jesus Christ.

Paul had tasted the love of God, and he relished it. He drank deeply of it, and he couldn't get enough. He could admonish the Ephesians, "That Christ may dwell in your hearts by faith; that ye, being rooted and grounded in love, may be able to comprehend with all saints what is the breadth, and length, and depth, and height; and to know the love of Christ, which passeth knowledge, that ye might be filled with the fulness of God" (Ephesians 3:17-19).

"Ocean of love"—that's the language Ellen White used as she plunged into the depths of this subject. "We have an inexhaustible storehouse, an ocean of love in the God of our salvation. He has placed in the hands of Christ all the treasures of the heavenly resources and says, 'All these are for man, in order to convince fallen, sinful man of My love; that there is no love in the universe but mine and that for his happiness I am working and will work.' " Continuing, she wrote, "One thing is impossible with God—the power of eclipsing the greatness of His gift in showing His love for fallen man, that He has given in Jesus. In this wonderful expression of His love He has given to fallen man, and to all the unfallen worlds, and to the universe of heaven, a clear evidence that there is no love but His love" (Ms. 83, 1895).

God Says, "I Love You"

With John 3:16, God tells every son and daughter of Adam, "I love you!" In 1 Corinthians 13, God teaches us to say the same thing to our neighbor, whoever he may be; not necessarily with those three powerful words, but with our actions. First Corinthians 13 is an inspired definition of love's behavior. It's really a job description! It's Paul's explanation of how the love of Christ really works in the lives of candidates for heaven, preparing them for another of God's gifts—eternal life!

This powerful "love chapter" is the rich, sweet, and creamy filling that fits between two chapters rich in theological lore, 1 Corinthians 12 and 1 Corinthians 14. This love chapter empowers the many gifts of the Holy Spirit described there. The love of God sweetens Paul's powerful list of the Spirit's endowments bestowed on church members. In verses 1 to 3 he makes it plain that no preacher can reap a harvest of precious souls unless his message erupts from a heart ablaze with the love of God. Nor can a prophet proclaim doctrine, reproof, correction, and instruction in righteousness (see 2 Timothy 3:16) without a divine burning love for God's erring people. Faith that moves mountains and zeal that is steadfast till death and closes the lips of the martyr are all fruitless and inconsequential, devoid of God's love. They're as empty as a drum and as noisy as "sounding brass."

If workers for God wish to succeed, they had better learn how to throw open the windows of their souls to receive the warm love of God, for the gospel machine runs on the fuel of love. Eloquent speech, brilliant logic, sound doctrine, powerful faith, and zealous labor are marks of distinction and dedication, but the marksmanship of love alone hits the target.

Love functions in a practical way. Its behavior is irreproachable and meant to be imitated. It makes a "people-person" out of a self-centered man or woman. "Before Christ," said Horace Wood, "a man loves things and uses people. After Christ he loves people and uses things."

Earth is nearest heaven when love is at work. This powerful, divine influence on the behavior of the saints of God results in the erection of temples in human flesh, lives that have been touched with the healing, converting power of God. Here divine principle is at work, not just ardor, emotion, and good impulses.

Paul's Behavior Patterns

Paul's behavior patterns of love are sixteen in number (see 1 Corinthians 13:4-7). The KJV is plain and understandable. However, as translated in different English versions, these elements of God's gift of love take on even broader significance. Note these brief examples:

Verse 4: "Love is gracious" (Riem); "This love of which I speak is slow to lose patience—it looks for a way of being constructive" (Phillips, revised edition); "Love knows no jealousy; love makes no parade" (Moffatt); "It does not put on airs" (Smith and Goodspeed).

Verse 5: "Is never rude" (Moffatt); "Love does not insist on its own way" (RSV); "Not quick to take offence. Love keeps no score of wrongs" (NEB).

Verse 6: "Does not gloat over other men's sins" (NEB); "but rejoices at the victory of truth" (Knox).

Verse 7: "Love knows no limit to its endurance, no end to its trust" (Phillips); "It keeps up hope in everything" (Williams); "It gives us power to endure everything" (Williams).

Verse 8: "Love will never come to an end" (NEB); "Love never disappears" (Moffatt); "Love shall never pass away" (Confraternity).

Since the days of William Tyndale, translators into English have used the word *love* in place of *charity*. Back in the days of Wycliffe, when he translated the Bible into English from Jerome's Latin Vulgate, he took the Latin word *carlites* (*love*) and translated it into *charity*. The word *charity* which in later years came to mean sympathy, pity, love for the underprivileged, etc., was surrendered in favor of the Greek *agape*, which, transformed by the life and ministry of Jesus, came to mean the love of heaven portrayed in us.

Keep in mind that Paul's sixteen points of love and light and righteousness are all embodied in the righteousness of Jesus Christ. "Righteousness is love, and love is the light and the life of God. The righteousness of God is embodied in Christ. We receive righteousness by receiving Him" (*Thoughts From the Mount of Blessing*, 18).

Righteousness, Holiness, and Love

To further illuminate this point, Ellen White wrote, "Righteousness is holiness, likeness to God, and 'God is love.' 1 John 4:16. It is conformity to the law of God, for 'all Thy commandments are righteousness' (Psalm 119:172), and 'love is the fulfilling of the law' (Romans 13:10)" (ibid.).

In light of this great truth, substitute *Jesus* for the word *charity* in 1 Corinthians 13:4-8, and it will read: *Jesus is longsuffering and kind. The Saviour does not envy. The Lord Jesus does not vaunt Himself, nor is He puffed up. He does not behave Himself unseemly. He seeks not His own. He is not easily provoked and gives no countenance to evil thinking. The Lord Jesus rejoices in the truth but never in iniquity. He bears all things, believes all things, hopes all things, endures all things. Jesus never fails.* (paraphrased)

The Saviour taught us the following: "Blessed are they which do hunger and thirst after righteousness: for they shall be filled" (Matthew 5:6); i.e., hunger and thirst for the love of God! In light of 1 Corinthians 13:4-8, all of these sixteen characteristics of love contained in the righteousness of Christ become ours when we receive Him. The love behavior of Jesus becomes the behavior of the saints.

The more we taste of the love of God, the more our souls cry for more and still more of it. Every morning, John Wesley's prayer was that God would "do it again" to keep him in the love of God.

Love, a Principle of Life

We say that God is love and correctly so, but is it proper to say that love is God? No. Love is a principle of life. This principle is embodied in Christ, but neither Christ nor God the Father nor the Holy Spirit is an intangible principle.

We say that God is light and that in Him there is no darkness at all. Correct. But light is not God. Light is a combination of waves. God is not such a combination. He is not a laboratory phenomenon. He is a being—a powerful and lovable being.

There are those who say God is nature and nature is God—pantheists. But nature is the thing God has made, not God Himself. It is God's power displayed in creation. Creation is not God. The created is not the Creator.

Christianity is not Christian science. Christianity is Christ, a lovely person who inhabits us through His Holy Spirit.

"Jesus Christ is everything to us," wrote Ellen White, "the first, the last, the best in everything. Jesus Christ, His Spirit, His character, colors everything; it is the warp and woof, the very texture of our entire being. The words of Christ are spirit and life. We cannot, then, center our thoughts upon self; it is no more we that live, but Christ that liveth in us, and He is the hope of glory. Self is dead, but Christ is a living Saviour. Continuing to look unto Jesus, we reflect His image to all around us" (*Messages to Young People*, 161).

So when we say "God is love" (1 John 4:8), we accept Him as a Being with all the behavioral traits of 1 Corinthians 13. He simply calls upon us to be like Him. "He is a perfect and holy example, given for us to imitate. We cannot equal the pattern; but we shall not be approved of God if we do not copy it and, according to the ability which God has given, resemble it" (*Testimonies for the Church*, 2:549).

But love today, as in times past, is interpreted by many to be an element in human life "having the power of physical sensation," a thing "perceived by the senses." People count their good feelings to be the ultimate joy of life. The right of every person to enjoy sexual expression, for example, is now termed "justice-love" by some proponents. They declare, "Where there is justice-love, sexual expression has ethical integrity." The meaning of this is that "what is" should be recognized by all of us, even the church, as acceptable—not what should be. Besides, the marriage state, they assert, should not interfere with sexual expression outside of marriage, whether it's homosexual or heterosexual. Even lesbian and homosexual persons who "love the Lord" should not be refused important church offices.

But the love of 1 Corinthians 13 is *agape* love, not *eros*, erotic love. Agape love does not behave itself unseemly. It thinks no evil and does not rejoice in error, but in the truth. Christian love never fails, but lust is always a failure. Solomon, king of Israel, turned from a life of sexual gratification to find the peace only God can give. He declared, "Though a sinner do evil an hundred times, and his days be prolonged, yet surely I know that it shall be well with them that fear God, which fear before him: but it shall not be well with the wicked" (Ecclesiastes 8:12, 13).

The Doctrine of Free Love

In the *Southern Watchman*, April 5, 1904, Ellen White wrote about certain persons who were deceived by the false doctrine of free love. "Presumptuous sins were committed, and unholy lusts were freely indulged by some, under the cloak of sanctification. The doctrine of spiritual free-love was advocated. We saw the fulfillment of the scripture 'that in the latter times some shall depart from the faith, giving heed to seducing spirits and doctrines of devils.' "

Under the umbrella of a mistaken concept of God's laws and the lowering of moral standards, bizarre sexual relations have come to be regarded as blessed of the Lord! According to *U.S. News & World Report* of June 10, 1991, today, one in five Americans loses his or her virginity before the age of fifteen. At least one-third of married men and women are having or have had an affair, lasting an average of nearly a year, and religion plays no role in shaping more than half of all Americans' opinions on such issues as sexuality and birth control. These conclusions were reported in a survey of two thousand men and women, authored by James Patterson and Peter Kim and published in a document titled "The Day America Told the Truth."

These startling facts are revolting, but the Christian can share the promises of God with the transgressor of God's laws.

Wash you, make you clean; put away the evil of your doings from before mine eyes; cease to do evil; learn to do well; seek judgment, relieve the oppressed, judge the fatherless, plead for the widow. Come now, and let us reason together, saith the Lord: though your sins be as scarlet, they shall be as white as snow; though they be red like crimson, they shall be as wool. If ye be willing and obedient, ye shall eat the good of the land (Isaiah 1:16-19).

Love for Those Who Need It

"Francis of Assisi was terrified of leprosy. And one day, full in the narrow path that he was traveling, he saw a leper! Instinctively his heart shrank back, recoiling shudderingly from the contamination of that loathsome disease. But then he rallied; and ashamed of himself, ran and cast his arms about the sufferer's neck and kissed him and passed on. A moment later he looked back, and there was no one there, only the empty road in the hot sunlight! All his days thereafter he was sure it was no leper, but Christ Himself whom he had met" (G. K. Chesterton).

It would seem that the perversion of love would effectually eliminate true love from the scene, but Paul tells us that faith, hope, and love will abide forever, while the carnal will perish. Prophecies may cease; earthly knowledge may fade away. Now we may know in part; then we shall know in the fullness of the light of eternity, but love never dies out. It remains as long as God remains and will conquer at last.

Yes, faith and hope likewise survive.

Faith will become clearer, stronger, richer, and more satisfying than we can imagine. Absolute dependence and happy confidence will find keener expression than ever before in our lives. *Hope* abides. At every turn in the road the believer can look expectantly for vistas of eternal beauty, for adventures to delight the heart, for evidence of the divine arm about him, for joys that are indescribable, for breath-taking moments of praise and awe and worship, and for soul-satisfying delights as the Saviour leads and lifts and blesses (Kyle M. Yates, *Preaching From Great Bible Chapters*, 50, 51.)

But like God Himself, love will continue on forever. And if love has become the ruling principle of our believing hearts, we, too, shall abide in God's joy-filled eternity!

Chapter 2:

Isaiah 53

THE MOUNT EVEREST OF MESSIANIC PROPHECIES

More than once my wife and I have flown from Washington, D.C., to Los Angeles. The 747s reach their cruising altitude at about 33,000 feet. The highest mountains between the two coastlines rise majestically into the Rockies—about 14,000 feet.

Let's suppose that Mount Everest, in the remote Himalayan mountains, was miraculously transported to the Rocky Mountain area. Our pilot would have to be very sensitive to our plane's altimeters, for Mount Everest rises about 29,000 feet above sea level, the highest landmark on planet Earth—only about 4,000 feet under the cruising altitude of the big jets.

For years, this snow-clad mountain resisted every effort to scale its formidable crest. Now, however, one climbing party after another has scaled the sharp, precipitous peaks. Flags of many countries are planted on its summit. Its mysteries and its awesome secrets have been opened up to the view of an admiring world.

There is also a glorious mountain peak in biblical literature, in Old Testament Messianic prophecy: Isaiah 53. Theologians view this mountain crest of prophetic revelation and foreknowledge as the supernal peak of truth about the suffering Son of God, Jesus Christ. It is history told in advance. These experts in biblical research have climbed other Old Testament Messianic peaks: Genesis 3:15; Deuteronomy 18:15-19; Psalm 2:6-12; 22:1-31; Daniel 9:24-27; Micah 4:8; 5:2; Zechariah 9:9; Malachi 3:1-3. As they have opened the pages of these inspired scriptures, they have breathtakingly discovered accurate portraits

13

of the historical Jesus from Bethlehem and Nazareth to Mount Golgotha and the Mount of Olives. They have seen in His life and death and resurrection unquestioned fulfillment—accurate information in prescient form. But not until they come to the Himalayas of Scripture—Isaiah's grand and glorious description of the suffering Messiah—do they discern the highest, the greatest, the most sublime unfolding of the character and work of the Son of God.

Who Is the Servant of the Lord?

Isaiah, the gospel prophet, makes several references to a person described as the servant of the Lord (see Isaiah 42:1-4; 52:13-15). In Isaiah 53:11 He is described as "my righteous servant [who] will justify many, and will bear their iniquities" (NIV). Who is this righteous servant of the Lord?

Jewish interpretations run the gamut from the historical view, which identifies the servant of the Lord as King Uzziah, King Hezekiah, or possibly King Josiah, to the autobiographical view, which makes Isaiah himself the servant of the Lord. Then there is the biographical view, which identifies this person as a contemporary of Isaiah's. The mystical view proposes that the "servant of the Lord" was Tammuz, a mythical god who died and rose again.

"According to the eschatological view, the Servant of God is the destined Redeemer, the Messiah. The approach is found at first in *Targum Jonathan* (in 42:1 and especially 51:13). But it has left few traces in Jewish exegesis in contrast to its important role in Christianity" (*Encyclopedia Judaic*, 9:66).

This confusion among Jewish scholars could be easily eliminated if Isaiah 53 were accepted at face value and compared with the life, death, and resurrection of the historical Jesus Christ. To admit this, however, would be tantamount to a confession and acceptance of Jesus as the Messiah of prophecy and history, an act that modern Israel as a whole will never accept, but that more and more individual Jews are accepting day by day.

Ellen G. White wrote:

Many who were convinced that Jesus was the Son of God were misled by the false reasoning of the priests and rabbis. These teachers had repeated with great effect the prophecies concerning the Messiah, that He would "reign in Mount Zion, and in Jerusalem, and before His ancients gloriously;" that He would "have dominion also from sea to sea, and from the river unto the ends of the earth." Isa. 24:23; Ps. 72:8. Then they made contemptuous comparisons between the glory here pictured and the humble appearance of Jesus. The very words of prophecy were so perverted as to sanction error. Had the people in sincerity studied the word for themselves, they would not have been misled. The sixty-first chapter of Isaiah testifies that Christ was to do the very work He did. Chapter fifty-three sets forth His rejection and sufferings in the world, and chapter fifty-nine describes the character of the priests and rabbis. . . .

Whoever will prayerfully study the Bible, desiring to know the truth, that he may obey it, will receive divine enlightenment. He will understand the Scriptures. "If any man willeth to do His will, he shall know of the teaching" (*The Desire of Ages*, 458, 459).

Converts From Israel

The earliest Christians, first century A.D., were Jews. These converts from Israel saw firsthand the fulfillment of the prophecy of Isaiah 53 in Jesus' crucifixion on Mount Golgotha. Peter, an eyewitness, in his first epistle wrote concerning the salvation of our souls, linking it to the event of Calvary. "The prophets who prophesied of the grace that was to be yours searched and inquired about this salvation; they inquired what person or time was indicated by the Spirit of Christ within them when predicting the sufferings of Christ and the subsequent glory" (1 Peter 1:10, 11, RSV).

In the final verses of Isaiah 52 and all the way through Isaiah 53, the language calls for the sacrifice of shed blood: Isaiah 52:14: visage and form marred; Isaiah 53:4: "stricken, smitten of God"; verse 5: "wounded," "bruised," "stripes"; verse 7: "oppressed," "afflicted," "lamb to the slaughter"; verse 8: "cut off out of the land of the living," "stricken"; verse 10: "put to grief," "soul an offering"; verse 11: "travail of . . . soul"; verse 12: "poured out his soul unto death."

Old Testament Prophecies Fulfilled

Here are Isaiah's, David's, and other Old Testament prophecies fulfilled in the life and death of the Messiah, Jesus Christ!

Ps. 69:9–Full of zeal John–2:17
Ps. 78:2–Teaching by parables–Matt. 13:34, 35
Isa. 35:5, 6–Working miracles–Matt. 11:4-6
Ps. 69:7, 9, 20–Bearing reproach–Rom. 15:3
Ps. 69:8–Rejected by His brethren–John 7:3-5
Ps. 69:4–Jews hated Him–John 15:24, 25
Ps. 118:22–Rejected by Jewish rulers–Mark 12:10-12
Ps. 2:1, 2–Jews and Gentiles combine against Him–Acts 4:27
Ps. 41:9–Betrayed by a friend–John 13:18, 21
Zech. 13:7–Forsaken by His disciples–Matt. 26:31, 56
Zech. 11:12–Sold for thirty pieces of silver–Matt. 26:15
Zech. 11:13–Potter's field bought with the money–Matt. 27:7
Ps. 22:14, 15–Intensity of His sufferings–Luke 22:42, 44
Isa. 53:6, 12–Suffered for others–Matt. 26:28
Isa. 53:7–Silent under abuse–Matt. 26:63; 27:12-14
Micah 5:1–Smitten on the cheek–Matt. 26:67; 27:30
Isa. 50:6–Spit upon and scourged–Mark 14:65
Ps. 22:16–Hands and feet nailed to the cross–John 19:18; 20:25
Ps. 22:1–Forsaken of God–Matt. 27:46
Ps. 22:7, 8–Was mocked–Matt. 27:29-44
Ps. 69:21–Given gall and vinegar–Matt. 27:34
Ps. 22:18–Lots cast for His vesture–Matt. 27:35
Isa. 53:12–Numbered with the transgressors–Mark 15:27, 28
Isa. 53:12–Made intercession for transgressors–Luke 23:34
Isa. 53:12–Poured out His soul unto death–Matt. 27:50
Ps. 34:20–Not one bone broken–John 19:33, 36
Zech 12:10–Was pierced–John 19:34, 37
Isa. 53:9–Buried with the rich–Matt. 27:57-60
Ps. 16:10–His flesh saw no corruption–Acts 2:31, 32

(Taken from Alonzo J. Werner, *Fundamentals of Bible Doctrine.*)

Reports have reached the rulers in Jerusalem that Jesus is approaching the city with a great concourse of people. But they have no welcome for the Son of God. In fear they go out to meet Him, hoping to disperse the throng. As the procession is about to descend the Mount of Olives, it is intercepted by the rulers. They inquire the cause of the tumultuous rejoicing. As they question, "Who is this?" the disciples, filled with the spirit of inspiration, answer this question. In eloquent strains they repeat the prophecies concerning Christ:

Adam will tell you, It is the seed of the woman that shall bruise the serpent's head.

Ask Abraham, he will tell you, It is "Melchizedek King of Salem," King of Peace. Gen. 14:18.

Jacob will tell you, He is Shiloh of the tribe of Judah.

Isaiah will tell you, "Immanuel," "Wonderful, Counselor, The mighty God, The everlasting Father, The Prince of Peace." Isa. 7:14; 9:6.

Jeremiah will tell you, The Branch of David, "the Lord our Righteousness." Jer. 23:6.

Daniel will tell you, He is the Messiah.

Hosea will tell you, He is "the Lord God of hosts; the Lord is His memorial." Hosea 12:5.

John the Baptist will tell you, He is "the Lamb of God, which taketh away the sin of the world" John 1:29.

The great Jehovah has proclaimed from His throne, "This is My beloved Son." Matt. 3:17.

We, His disciples, declare, This is Jesus, the Messiah, the Prince of life, the Redeemer of the world.

And the prince of the powers of darkness acknowledges Him, saying "I know Thee who Thou art, the Holy One of God." Mark 1:24 (*The Desire of Ages*, 578, 579).

Behold the Lamb of God

If Isaiah the prophet had been resurrected at the time Jesus was born in Bethlehem, he would have recognized Jesus as the Messiah, the subject of his uncannily accurate prediction. There would have been no doubt in his mind. He would have publicly proclaimed, "Here He is, the suffering Messiah about whom I prophesied!" Like John the Baptist, he would have proclaimed, "Behold the Lamb of God, which taketh away the sin of the world."

Not so the disciples. Even after His death and resurrection, they still doubted that He was the Messiah. They still held to the Soldier-Deliverer idea promoted by the priests. They wanted no suffering Son of God.

Come and observe with me now as we accompany Jesus and the two disciples on the walk to Emmaus. The resurrected Lord is not recognized by these two sorrowing men. Jesus listens as they relate painfully "how the chief priests and our rulers delivered him [Jesus of Nazareth] to be condemned to death, and have crucified him" (Luke 24:20).

We observe as Jesus holds Himself back from speaking. He listens to the sorrowful confession of their trust "that it had been He [the Messiah], which should have redeemed Israel." Whereupon Jesus "said unto them, O fools, and slow of heart to believe all that the prophets have spoken: Ought not Christ to have suffered these things, and to enter into his glory?" (Luke 24:21, 25, 26).

Listen now to the revealing prophecy of Isaiah. "Who hath believed our report? and to whom is the arm of the Lord revealed" (Isaiah 53:1). Or as we have it in the Living Bible, "But, oh, how few believe it! Who will listen? To whom will God reveal his saving power?"

Believe what? Believe what Isaiah had written in the preceding verses: "They shall see my Servant beaten and bloodied, so disfigured one would scarcely know it was a person standing there" (Isaiah 52:15, TLB).

If the disciples were bewildered by the events that had so recently occurred and still had doubts about the Messianic character of Jesus, certainly the suffering Son of God entertained no such misgivings! He recognized in Himself the Messiah of Isaiah's prediction.

"Beginning at Moses and all the prophets, he expounded unto them in all the scriptures the things concerning *himself*" (Luke 24:27, emphasis added).

Did Jesus know before He appeared on earth that He would encounter such bitter hatred from His own people that He would be taken away and crucified on a hill between two malefactors? Indeed, He did know it. He knew it from the perspective of eternity. Indeed, it was He Himself who inspired Isaiah to write his fifty-third chapter (see 1 Peter 1:10, 11).

The Cross and the Resurrection

In Psalm 40:6-10 we see how Jesus foretold the end of the Jewish system of animal sacrifices. He predicted, also, His own arrival on the scene of prophetic fulfillment as humanity's Saviour—the cross of shame and the miraculous resurrection.

Matthew, Mark, Luke, and John provide the clearest historical account of that "never-to-be-forgotten experience." But Isaiah's prophecy matches the historical record! One author has said:

Did it ever occur to you to go to Isaiah for the most unusual, the most exciting, and the most gripping description of that scene? You will find that this chapter is the keenest interpretation of the events in that dramatic moment in the history of redemption. This chapter sounds more like a New Testament evangelist than an Old Testament *prophet* (Yates, 85).

Isaiah prophesied: "He was despised, and we esteemed him not" (Isaiah 53:3). Mark records the historical evidence: "It is written of the Son of man, that he must suffer many things, *and be set at nought*" (Mark 9:12, emphasis added). Isaiah prophesied the wounding and bruising of the Messiah for the iniquities of the people (see Isaiah 53:5-7, 10). Philip, one of Jesus' disciples, recognized in the Saviour the fulfillment of the promise, and he testified to the eunuch of Ethiopia: "He was led as a sheep to the slaughter; and like a lamb dumb before his shearer, so opened he not his mouth" (Acts 8:32).

Isaiah prophesied:

> It pleased the Lord to bruise him; he hath put him to grief: when thou shalt make his soul an offering for sin, he shall see his seed, he shall prolong his days, and the pleasure of the Lord shall prosper in his hand. He shall see of the travail of his soul, and shall be satisfied: by his knowledge shall my righteous servant justify many; for he shall bear their iniquities (Isaiah 53:10, 11).

Peter declared, "You know that you were ransomed from the futile ways inherited from your fathers, not with perishable things such as silver or gold, but with the precious blood of Christ, like that of a lamb without blemish or spot. . . . He was destined before the foundation of the world but was made manifest at the end of the times for your sake" (1 Peter 1:18-20, RSV). Peter knew where the credit for human salvation belonged.

The Precious Blood of Christ

Why was the blood of Christ so precious? Dwight L. Moody, the evangelist, put it this way: "First, because it redeems us. . . . If gold and silver could have redeemed us, do you not think that God would have created millions of worlds full of gold? It would have been an easy matter for Him. But we are not redeemed by such corruptible things but by the precious blood of Christ" (Ralph Turnbull, ed., *The Best of Dwight L. Moody,* Grand Rapids, Mich.: Baker Book House, 1991).

In Calcutta, India, I visited the Temple of Kali—a Hindu sanctuary that on the day of my visit was packed with restless worshipers. I had an eerie feeling as I walked through the crowded worship hall. Outside in the courtyard I observed a wealthy Hindu couple who had brought the kid of a goat to be sacrificed to Kali, the avenging goddess. The priest accepted the gift, drew from his sheath a heavy Indian knife, and severed the head of the innocent creature. It was a swift and cruel blow. A pool of blood gathered in the stones. The husband and wife rushed forward, dipped their eager fingers in the warm blood, and applied it to their foreheads. This was the way they had been taught to obtain release from guilt and the wrath of Kali.

Centuries before, the apostle Paul wrote to the Hebrews that "without shedding of blood is no remission" (Hebrews 9:22). But Paul understood that remission of sins did not come through animal sacrifices, "the blood of goats and calves, but by his own blood" (Hebrews 9:12). The blood of Jesus, not the blood of beasts of the field, purges the conscience. Jesus is the antitype of the Jewish animal sacrifices, and without faith in His blood, shed for our sins, remission is beyond our reach.

The Gospel Will Suffice

There are some who seek to earn pardon through their own good behavior. "I don't do anything wrong," they say. "I pay my bills. I don't beat my kids. I'm a good husband and a good neighbor. I belong to the Optimist Club. I go to church on Easter Sunday. What's wrong with that? What more can I do?"

They are like the little boy in juvenile court protesting charges against him. "I ain't no bad kid," he affirms, "I washes my face every day." That was his view of acceptable morality. That was all that God or humans should expect from him.

Atonement by proxy is acceptable only if the proxy is Jesus. No kid, no goat, no good deed—past, present, or future, is acceptable atonement. As E. Stanley Jones put it, "Jesus is the supreme necessity."

Why is the blood of Christ so precious? A further reason is that the blood of Jesus brings us closer to God. "Now in Christ Jesus ye who sometimes were far off were made nigh by the blood of Christ" (Ephesians 2:13).

Moody, who'd preached widely in North America and in England, declared, "I can go to any community where I am an entire stranger, and preach this doctrine of atonement, and get better acquainted in 24 hours than I could if I talked about old Socrates and Plato for 24 years. . . . Hold up the cross and you'll get the true believers around it in a little while, but go to preaching science and botany and astronomy and metaphysics and you get them all quarreling. The cross is a drawing power. The cross is a center. Bring people nigh to it and you bring them nigh to each other."

Peace Between God and Humanity

The blood of Jesus is precious, also, because it makes peace between humanity and God and God and humanity. "Having made peace through the blood of his cross" (Colossians 1:20).

In a sense, Jesus made out His will when He died for us. Moody made much of this in his sermons. When Jesus died, He committed His spirit to His Father; to Joseph of Arimathaea, He willed His body; His mother was assigned to John, the son of Zebedee; and then to His disciples, He said, "Peace I leave with you, my peace I give unto you: not as the world giveth, give I unto you. Let not your heart be troubled, neither let it be afraid" (John 14:27).

The Lord Jesus holds the wealth of the world in His hands. The silver and the gold and the cattle upon a thousand hills are His, yet He does not bequeath to His followers material riches, but spiritual treasures. As it is impossible for us to be redeemed by silver and gold, so it is that His redemption, the reward of His shed blood, does not consist of gifts of money and houses and lands to His children. Peace and joy and a knowledge of sins forgiven are their greatest treasures. Peace with God brings the greatest joy in the world, the most valuable possession.

G. Franklin Allee said, "In the New Testament there are 290 references to the love of God, 290 times when God has declared His love for man. But in the same chapters and same verses there are more than 1,300 references to the atonement; 1,300 assurances that salvation can be had through the blood of Christ."

John the Beloved declared, "If we walk in the light, as he is in the light, we have fellowship one with another, and the blood of Jesus Christ his Son cleanseth us from all sin" (1 John 1:7).

One day a preacher was speaking from this text. An atheist in the audience stood to his feet, interrupting him and questioning, "How can blood cleanse sin?"

The preacher hardly knew what to say, but the Lord gave him the words, and he countered with, "How can water quench thirst?"

The infidel replied, "I don't know, but I know that it does."

The preacher answered by saying, "Neither do I know how

the blood of Jesus cleanses sin, but I know that it does."

"The cross stands alone, a great center in the world. It does not find friends, but it makes them. It creates its own agencies" (Ellen G. White Comments, *SDA Bible Commentary*, 5:1138).

In the Caribbean islands years ago, workers in the cane fields brought the cut cane to the factory to be crushed. The burnt stalks were pushed through the grinder. The cane juice gathered in a large vat, blackened by the stalks that earlier had been burned to destroy the leaves. A pailful of calf's blood would be poured into the vat of cane juice. Immediately, the dirt and the impurities were attracted to the blood, and the cane juice was cleansed. It was the blood that did the trick. The coagulated material, with all the dirt and impurities attached, was carefully removed from the vat, and the pure juice, cleansed and purified, remained.

There is no other way to be cleansed from the stigma, the guilt, the power of sin. The stain is removed. Jesus washes clean with the blood. Since the blood is the life, the repentant sinner receives new life and power from the cleansing blood of Jesus. In view of the fact that Christ has cleansed our sins, don't you think we ought to be the happiest people in the world?

Boldness to Approach God

In Ephesians 3, Paul addresses the issue of God's eternal purpose, stating that through Christ Jesus our Lord, we can have boldness and access with confidence.

Boldness is not presumption. King Uzziah of Judah entered the sacred temple to perform a work assigned exclusively to the priests. He was struck with leprosy, from which he suffered until he died. We do not follow Christ in His work in the heavenly sanctuary with such presumption, for when we enter by His merits, clothed in His righteousness, washed in His blood, we have access. "Having therefore, brethren, boldness to enter into the holiest by the blood of Jesus, by a new and living way, which he hath consecrated for us, through the veil" (Hebrews 10:19, 20).

Jesus' Triumph and Satisfaction

Paul testifies of Jesus' triumph (see Philippians 2:5-11).

"In what could the Messiah find satisfaction? He would be exceedingly happy when He saw the full glory that would come to the Father. He would rejoice when He saw the uncounted millions coming in sincere faith to become new creatures. How happy He could become as He looked upon uncounted 'trophies of grace.' He would shout for joy as He recognized the beautiful character produced in His own followers. We do not wonder that He is 'satisfied' " (Kyle M. Yates, *Preaching From Great Bible Chapters*, 98).

So because of the salvation provided on the hill of Golgotha, we may someday soon stand in God's kingdom and join the other redeemed as they sing of Moses and the Lamb, who was slain for our redemption.

Your heavenly Father will take from you the garments defiled by sin. In the beautiful parabolic prophecy of Zechariah, the high priest Joshua, standing clothed in filthy garments before the angel of the Lord, represents the sinner. And the word is spoken by the Lord, "Take away the filthy garments from him. And unto him He said, Behold I have caused thine iniquity to pass from thee, and I will clothe thee with change of raiment. . . . So they set a fair miter upon his head, and clothed him with garments." Zech. 3:4, 5. Even so God will clothe you with "the garments of salvation," and cover you with "the robe of righteousness." Isa. 61:10. "Though ye have lien among the pots, yet shall ye be as the wings of a dove covered with silver, and her feathers with yellow gold." Ps. 68:13 (*Christ's Object Lessons*, 206).

Chapter 3:

Hebrews 11

THE BIBLICAL HALL OF FAME

The eleventh chapter of Hebrews contains one of the most encouraging messages in the Bible. "When we are . . . convinced that we are undone and of unclean lips, we consider the men and women of the eleventh chapter of Hebrews. This changes all. . . . We're given a view of what God has done for others and we take courage. If Gideon, with a little faith, obtained a good report, then there is hope for us. If Rahab prevailed, then God can forgive our sins also. If Samson at last made his peace with God, He will not turn us away. If David was forgiven, then we may have hope. If Jacob at last gained heaven, we need not despair. . . . We thank God for the eleventh chapter of Hebrews. The chapter that not only speaks of peace but instills hope in every breast" (M. L. Andreason, *That Hope*, 508).

"And how did Gideon and Rahab and Samson and David and Jacob and all the other heroes and heroines of Hebrews 11 obtain victory? Answer: 'By faith.' The eleventh chapter of the letter to the Hebrews may be described as a record of witnesses to the truth of a principle. This principle is found in the tenth chapter where it occurs as a quotation from the prophecy of Habakkuk: 'My righteous one shall live by faith,' or in the form found in the King James Version: 'The just shall live by faith.' These words are also found quoted in Paul's letter to the Romans, and in his letter to the Galatians" (G. Campbell Morgan, *Great Chapters of the Bible*, 312).

So the New Testament concept of faith living and faith doing is borrowed from an Old Testament principle, equally important in the Old and the New Testament.

A Lesson From History

All the minor prophets, including Habakkuk, were over-whelmed with sorrow because of the iniquities of their Israelite kinsmen. God was forced, therefore, to "raise up the Chaldeans, that bitter and hasty nation, which shall march through the breadth of the land, to possess the dwellingplaces that are not their's [sic]. They are terrible and dreadful" (Habakkuk 1:6, 7).

Though the Chaldeans became the rod of God's anger against an apostate people, they in turn became puffed up with pride and self-exaltation. Habakkuk knew that this would happen and warned, "Behold, his soul which is lifted up is not upright in him" (Habakkuk 2:4). He knew that God would punish the Chaldeans, though He had used them to discipline His people. All of this Habakkuk saw in vision, and he wrote it out in Habakkuk 2:1-3. But he added this triumphant note, "The just shall live by his faith." By faith, the prophet could look ahead and see that God was still in charge and that He would deliver His people from captivity and provide life and length of days to those who should live by faith.

Habakkuk closes his book by writing, "I will rejoice in the Lord, I will joy in the God of my salvation. The Lord God is my strength, and he will make my feet like hinds' feet, and he will make me to walk upon mine high places" (Habakkuk 3:18, 19). Faith always produces a note of triumph. Faith is the victory that overcomes the world and all the enemies of Jehovah. It is the saving link that connects believing humanity with God.

Faith Defined

But what is faith? "Faith is the substance of things hoped for, the evidence of things not seen" (Hebrews 11:1). Faith is the means by which we obtain a good report (verse 2) from God. Verse 1 is the only definition of faith found in the Holy Scriptures. The Bible tells of men and women who have lived by faith, done great exploits for God by faith, and triumphed by faith, but here faith is explained.

"In this definition two spheres of action are named, those

namely of 'things hoped for,' and 'things not seen.' 'Things hoped for' are things not yet possessed, but desired and expected. 'Things not seen' are things beyond the sphere of the possible demonstration by the senses" (G. Campbell Morgan, *Great Chapters of the Bible*, 313).

The American Standard Version (ASV) translates verse 1, "Now faith is assurance of things hoped for." Weymouth has it, "Now faith is a confident assurance of that for which we hope." Again, "But faith forms a solid ground for what is hoped for" (Berkeley). It is "a conviction of things not seen" (ASV). "And makes us certain of realities we do not see" (NEB).

Here's Martin Luther's definition of faith:

> There are two kinds of believing: first, a believing about God, which means that I believe that what is said of God is true. This faith is rather a form of knowledge than of faith. There is, secondly, a believing in God which means I put my trust in Him, give myself up to thinking that I can have dealings with Him, and believe without any doubt that He will be and do to me according to things said of Him. Such faith which throws itself upon God, whether in life or in death, alone makes a Christian.

So faith, true living faith, is dynamic. It goes beyond the static kind of belief that distinguishes Satan and many professors of religion. "Thou believest that there is one God; thou doest well: the devils also believe, and tremble" (James 2:19).

Hebrews 11 is a record taken from church history that describes how faith acts by love and purifies the faithful actor. Indeed, faith is so important that "it is impossible to please" God without it. "For he that cometh to God must believe that he is, and that he is a rewarder of them that diligently seek him" (verse 6).

It is said that Mohammed once overheard one of his followers say, "I will loose my camel and commit it to God." "Friend," said the prophet, "tie thy camel and commit it to God." Faith—a saying of belief—must be accompanied by works—a doing of belief!

The Breathtaking Account

Hebrews 11 also gives brilliant examples of how faith works. The splendid exploits of the characters in this breathtaking account were wrought by God through faith actors.

Beginning with Abel—son of the first human couple and the first victim of murder—and ending with the godly prophet Samuel, the author of Hebrews plucks out of this stellar hall of fame sixteen models for emulation who, like Paul, could say, "Follow me as I follow Christ" (see Hebrews 11:4-32).

What can your faith do? Faith is boundless (John 11:21-27); precious (2 Peter 1:1); unfeigned (1 Timothy 1:5); venturing (Matthew 14:28, 29); great (Matthew 8:10).

Moses' faith could see God (Hebrews 11:24, 28); Abraham's could see the Promised Land (Romans 4:16-22); the three Hebrews in the fiery furnace could risk life for God (Daniel 3:13-26); Enoch could please God (Hebrews 11:5); Job could trust God in affliction (Job 19:25-27).

And how did these spirit-filled men and women acquire the graces of the soul? What distinguished them? How was it that they received righteousness, obtained the promises, shut the mouths of lions, put to flight the alien armies, subdued kingdoms, and endured privation and torture for Christ's sake? How did it all happen? The answer lies in that powerful force provided by God called faith—a word used twenty-three times in Hebrews 11.

Note carefully how faith exploded into active obedience to the word of the Lord:

1. "By faith Noah, being warned of God of things not seen as yet . . . prepared an ark" (verse 7). The ark was prepared for the rescue mission, but the rain and the flood were "not seen as yet." "Why the boat?" people asked. There was no rain—no sea of waters. It was a faith adventure, pure and simple. And time proved it was the right thing to do.

2. "By faith Abraham, when he was called to go out . . . obeyed; and he went out, not knowing whither he went" (verse 8). Before you jump, we say, be sure you know where you are going to land—this is conventional wisdom. But faith—wisdom—says, God knows, so trust Him and go ahead! Abraham went ahead

and discovered Canaan, a figure of the better world, "for he looked for a city which hath foundations, whose builder and maker is God" (verse 10). He became the father of all the faith children of God through the centuries (see also verses 17-19)!

3. "By faith [Moses] forsook Egypt, not fearing the wrath of the king: for he endured, as seeing him who is invisible" (verse 27). Moses heard God's voice calling him to leadership—to the emancipation of His people from Egyptian bondage, but he could not see God. He chose, rather, to identify himself with a nation of slaves than to enjoy the pleasures of sin for a season. What a faith model for the modern Christian, who likewise must forsake the Egypt of sin and embark on the journey to Canaan!

These remarkable characters lived in Old Testament times. They didn't have the example of Jesus Christ, the incarnate Son of God, to follow, as we do. The Model existed in prophecy, not history. All these godly people, and others equally notable, became like Jesus in life and character, and Paul, inspired by the Holy Spirit, links them together with his own generation and to this, the last age of human history. Here are his words: "That they without us should not be made perfect" (Hebrews 11:40). That is, God had foreseen some better thing for us Christians that these model saints of the past could not achieve—completeness. The church in Old Testament times is linked with the church in New Testament times, showing oneness and unity—like the temple of God composed of lively stones but incomplete in Old Testament times, which cannot be finished until the remnant church of God is ready for the second advent.

Besides the sixteen heroes and heroines of faith in Hebrews 11 who are typical, think of Caleb, a senior citizen, the contemporary of Joshua and Moses, who had faith in the Lord's promise, delivered over four decades before, that he would receive an inheritance of land in Canaan.

On his eighty-fifth birthday, this unsinkable, unflappable old veteran's faith rang out, "Give me this mountain" (see Joshua 14:6-12). Joshua consented, and so Caleb, with his Judean forces, drove out the Anakim from the hills of Hebron and claimed his prize.

Think, too, of the Ethiopian eunuch who, having heard the

prophecy of Isaiah 53 explained to him by the apostle Philip (see Acts 8:26-39), claimed the Saviour, Jesus, as Lord and Redeemer and was baptized.

Book of Better Things

Now the inspired apostle asserts that "God [has] provided some better thing for us, that they without us should not be made perfect." What better thing is intended? The book of Hebrews is a book of "better things"—a better sacrifice, a better priesthood, a better covenant, better promises—all the way through the book of Hebrews the apostle offers something better (even someone better—Jesus) than could be provided in the historical records of the Old Testament.

Christ as Sacrifice, Priest, and King is the "something better" of this remarkable treatise by Paul. Something better is indeed the watchword of life, the law of all victorious living. There's always something better than we had before. But Jesus is more than a "something." He is the "Somebody" of all Scripture.

Matthew, Mark, Luke, and John tell the wonderful story of Him in whom all our hopes center. And in this Christ-filled book of Hebrews, the apostle invites us to "consider him" (see Hebrews 12:1-5). Even a pagan judge called upon to preside at the trial of Jesus declared, "I find no fault in him" (John 19:4). And Peter, a contemporary of Jesus and an observer of His perfect life, exclaimed,

Even hereunto were ye called: because Christ also suffered for us, leaving us an example, that ye should follow his steps: who did no sin, neither was guile found in his mouth: who, when he was reviled, reviled not again; when he suffered, he threatened not; but committed himself to him that judgeth righteously: who his own self bare our sins in his own body on the tree, that we, being dead to sins, should live unto righteousness: by whose stripes ye were healed. For ye were as sheep going astray; but are now returned unto the Shepherd and Bishop of your souls (1 Peter 2:21-25).

The superiority of Christ, the model and antitype, is contrasted with self-righteous rituals of the Jews. Indeed, the righteousness and exploits of all the godly characters of Hebrews 11 were obtained by trusting Jesus and looking forward to His example. So we obtain our righteousness by looking back to the cross of Christ. In either case, however, we can claim holiness only in our human sphere, while He, the Creator and God, knew it in the sphere of the divine.

Paul's method of presenting Christ as a Person better than angels and better than the best of humans was undoubtedly learned as a student in Hebrew schools. Hillel, eminent liberal theologian of those days, advanced the principle of comparing the minor to the major. Paul here uses a similar method, moving from people and things on earth to Christ and things in heaven.

Faith Has a Cause

Faith is the spring of dynamic action in good works. But faith is produced by a threefold cause: (1) Reading the Scriptures (John 20:30, 31; (2) preaching the Word (John 17:20); (3) hearing the gospel (Acts 15:7). Faith is born as a consequence of one or all of these stimulating forces. Faith is confidence in the testimony of God. Throughout the Scriptures, in both the Old and New Testaments, we see faith springing forth in good works as a consequence of being challenged by the Word of the Lord.

By exposure to God's Word, faith is ignited to become a fire of blazing hope and expectancy. But confidence must be rooted in the promises of God and not in the crackling of that fire.

Faith and feeling are as distinct as the east is from the west. Faith is not dependent on feeling. We must earnestly cry to God in faith, feeling or no feeling, and then live our prayers. Our assurance and evidence is God's word, and after we have asked we must believe without doubting. I praise Thee, O God, I praise Thee. Thou hast not failed me in the performance of Thy word. Thou has revealed Thyself unto me, and I am Thine to do Thy will (Ellen G. White Comments, *SDA Bible Commentary*, 6:1073).

The Story of Two People

As we study the biographical sketches of the Word of God, we learn that the Bible is really the story of two people repeated over and over again. Its message can be reduced to the experience of two men or two women: (1) the believing party, who accepts and acts upon the Word of God; (2) the unbelieving party, who rejects the testimony of God and acts out a purely human course of action.

Abel's faith was born of the creative word by which he had been instructed. Cain's faith was tied to a rationale created by his own unbelieving mind. Abel's God-centered faith cost him his life. Cain's self-centered faith cost him his soul. Here is an illustration of "The Story of Two People."

> The two brothers erected their altars alike, and each brought an offering. Abel presented a sacrifice from the flock, in accordance with the Lord's directions. "And the Lord had respect unto Abel and to his offering." Fire flashed from heaven and consumed the sacrifice. But Cain, disregarding the Lord's direct and explicit command, presented only an offering of fruit. There was no token from heaven to show that it was accepted. Abel pleaded with his brother to approach God in the divinely prescribed way, but his entreaties only made Cain the more determined to follow his own will. As the eldest, he felt above being admonished by his brother, and despised his counsel (*Patriarchs and Prophets*, 71, 72).

Yes, the Bible is the story of King David and King Saul; of King Jehoshaphat and King Ahab; of Mordecai and Haman; of Ruth and Orpah; of Peter and Judas; of Paul and Demas.

And to make the story of two people more Adventist oriented, it is the story of A. G. Daniells, an early president of the General Conference of Seventh-day Adventists, and D. M. Canright, who wanted to be president but never made it. A. G. Daniells believed the word of the Lord and the messages that came from God's servant, Ellen G. White. D. M. Canright refused to accept the counsel and reaped tragic results.

And what did David and Jehoshaphat and Mordecai and Ruth and Peter and A. G. Daniells have in common? The answer is clear—*faith*! They had respect for the Lord's commands and His promises.

But Saul stumbled at the command of God; Ahab despised the word of the prophet; Orpah lacked the faith of her sister-in-law, Ruth; Demas forsook the apostle Paul, having loved this present world; D. M. Canright could not tolerate the discipline of discipleship, and he was too ambitious.

Approaching the End of Time

The end of time is rapidly approaching. Hebrews 11 was written for us to contemplate. But read also Hebrews 10:35-39. Paul was here addressing Hebrew Christians, who were expecting Christ to return, as did the Thessalonians and other early believers. But many at that time in the first century were in need of patience. Some were on the verge of apostasy. "For yet a little while," wrote the apostle, "and he that shall come will come, and will not tarry." He urged them not to draw back, for if they continued to believe, and rely on the promises by faith, they would save their souls.

But these verses in Hebrews 10:35-39 are provided for end-time Christians also, for the second coming is nearer than for the apostolic believers. When the author of Hebrews wrote this treatise about the year A.D. 68, the destruction of Jerusalem was near, even at the door. It was end time for them. The city perished under the assaults of Titus in A.D. 70. To prevent apostasy, Paul sent the Hebrew Christians the book of Hebrews to explain that the end of the Jerusalem temple and of Judaic rites and ceremonies was near at hand. But something better was to take the place of old Hebrew rituals. The temple in heaven was to be the object of their devotions and dedication. The Lord and Saviour was there as High Priest, after the order of Melchizedek. He would return some day as King of kings and Lord of lords. Until He did return, they were to keep looking up. They were to look back to the cross of Calvary, up to the throne of glory, and ahead to the cloud of His second coming.

Cloud With a Silver Lining

The second advent disappointments of the spring and fall of 1844 were perfectly anticipated by the author of Hebrews (see Hebrews 10:35-39). Adventists today stand at the threshold of events that answer to the destruction of Jerusalem. We need patience, for 150 years have passed since the Millerite movement of 1844, and Christ has not yet returned. Hebrews 11 is a cloud with a silver lining wrapped around the people to assure them that God did not desert the heirs of faith in Bible times or in the 1840s, nor will He abandon the heroes of faith today, for He will accomplish the fulfillment of all His prophecies. Consider Him, lest you become weary and faint in your minds.

Now, what was it the ancients did to account for their transformed lives and extraordinary exploits for God? Paul tells us that it was "by faith" and "through faith." So will we triumph at last! "Wherefore seeing we also are compassed about with so great a cloud of witnesses, let us lay aside every weight, and the sin which doth so easily beset us, and let us run with patience the race that is set before us" (Hebrews 12:1).

"The activity of faith is not over, it is still proceeding, and will continue to do so until the purposes of God are fully realized in human history, and that by faith, and by faith alone, can we be workers together with Him towards that consummation" (G. Campbell Morgan, *Great Chapters of the Bible*, 318).

"Without us [they] should not be made perfect" (Hebrews 11:39).

In ancient times, Abraham, Isaac, Jacob, Moses with his meekness and wisdom, and Joshua with his varied capabilities, were all enlisted in God's service. The music of Miriam, the courage and piety of Deborah, the filial affection of Ruth, the obedience and faithfulness of Samuel, the stern fidelity of Elijah, the softening, subduing influence of Elisha—all were needed. So now all upon whom God's blessing has been bestowed are to respond by actual service; every gift is to be employed for the advancement of His kingdom and the glory of His name (*Christ's Object Lessons*, 301).

Chapter 4:

Genesis 1

IN THE BEGINNING

"In the beginning God created the heaven(s) and the earth" (Genesis 1:1). "(Prepared, formed, fashioned,) and created" (Amplified Bible).

The book of Genesis, along with many other of the sixty-six books of the Bible, brings into sharp focus one of the most important realities of religion—the origin of life—creation!

Genesis 1 is a battlefield for old-time controversies between Bible-believing Christians on the one hand, and scientists, skeptics, atheists, and various shades of rationalists on the other. Many of the latter, who seek in different ways and in different degrees to explain the universe, some with, some without God, argue that matter is eternal. Speaking contrary to this point, the *SDA Bible Commentary* says, "If this be true, and if matter has the power to evolve, first into the simplest forms of life and then into the more complex, until man is reached, God is indeed unnecessary" (1:207). But if God—a personal God—is unnecessary in creation or the origin of life, who is to take His place: an idol made of wood or stone or a man-made theory, such as evolution?

According to a new Gallup Poll, 47 percent of Americans believe the strict creationist view, that God created humans pretty much in their present form at one time within the last ten thousand years. Forty percent of all Americans accept the centrist (modified) view that humans have developed over millions of years from less advanced forms of life, but God has guided this process, including human beings' creation. Nine percent maintain the naturalist view, namely, that humans have developed over millions of years from less advanced forms of life, but God has no part in this process (see *Newsweek*, 23 Dec. 1991). So the vast majority of Americans cannot divorce God from the origin of humans and this planet.

The biblical view is represented by the following comment by Ellen White: "God spoke, and His words created His works in the natural world. God's creation is but a reservoir of means made ready for Him to employ instantly to do His pleasure. . . . Infinite love—how great it is! God made the world to enlarge heaven. He desires a large family of created intelligences" (*SDA Bible Commentary*, 1:1081; see also Psalm 136:3-9). This planet and humankind upon it are a necessity in order to reveal God's creation plan, but "the work of creation cannot be explained by science. What science can explain the mystery of life?" (*The Ministry of Healing*, 414).

Theories of Origin

"It would be much easier to discuss how life didn't originate than how it did," said J. D. Bernal of Great Britain years ago. Theories of origin of the earth and of life on this planet are never held with any degree of satisfaction except by the Christian who finds security in Genesis 1 and the idea that life must come from a Lifegiver, a heavenly Creator-God.

Note the sublime biblical language penned by a humble farmer-prophet, through whom the Creator identifies Himself:

Seek Him that maketh the Pleiades and Orion,
And turneth the shadow of death into the morning,
And maketh the day dark with night (Amos 5:8, ARV).
He that formeth the mountains, and createth the wind,
And declareth unto man what is His thought (Amos 4:13, ARV).
He that buildeth His spheres in the heaven,
And hath founded His arch (Noyes) in the earth (Amos 9:6, ARV, margin).
He that calleth for the waters of the sea,
And poureth them out upon the face of the earth;

Jehovah is His name (Amos 9:6, ARV).

The Creator was not indebted to preexisting matter in His marvelous work of creation. The words of Genesis, "God said," introduce the divine command responsible for the historic events of the six days of Creation (see Genesis 1: 3, 6, 9, 11, 14, 20, 24). Each command came charged with a creative energy that transformed a planet "without form, and void" into a paradise. "He spake . . . and it stood fast" (Psalm 33:9). Truly, "the worlds were framed by the word of God" (Hebrews 11:3). "By faith we understand that the universe was formed at God's command, so that what is seen was not made out of what was visible" (Hebrews 11:3, NIV). At times God did use preexisting matter— e.g., Adam and the beasts were formed of the earth, and Eve was made from Adam's rib (Genesis. 2:7, 19, 22).

Augustine declared his belief that "God hath made all things out of nothing: because, even though the world hath been made of some material, that very same material hath been made out of nothing."

Literal Twenty-four-Hour Days

The first day and all the other days of Creation week were literal twenty-four-hour periods, not symbols of long time periods (Genesis 1:5, 8, 13, 19, 23, 31; 2:1-3). Morning equals day; evening equals night. The two periods together equal a twenty-four-hour day.

The tenacity with which so many commentators cling to the idea that the days of creation were long periods of time, even thousands of years, largely finds its explanation in the fact that they attempt to make the inspired creation record agree with the theory of evolution. Geologists and biologists have taught men to believe that this earth's early history covers millions of years, in which the geological formations were slowly taking shape and living species were evolving. Throughout its sacred pages the Bible contradicts this evolution theory. The belief in a divine and instantaneous creation as the result of words spoken by God stands in complete opposition to the theory held by the majority of scientists and many theologians today that the world and all upon it came into being through a slow process of evolution lasting for untold ages (*SDA Bible Commentary,* 1:211).

In his recent book, *A Brief History of Time*, the noted British physicist, Stephen Hawking, raises the question as to whether the worlds of science and religion are really at odds or are compatible over this question. He projects the thought that with new discoveries in physics, there is now reason to believe that religious tradition can be supported by science.

But science has come up short with its evaluation of life's origins and development. Unaided by divine revelation, it must still theorize and guess, and its views are continually changing. Note this comment by Dr. Gerald L. Schroeder:

> Since the monumental "Conference on Macro-Evolution" was held in Chicago in 1980, there has been a total re-evaluation of life's origins and development. In regard to the Darwinian theory of evolution, the world-famous paleontologist of the American Museum of Natural History, Dr. Niles Eldridge, unequivocally declared, "The pattern that we were told to find for the last one hundred and twenty years *does not exist.* There is now overwhelmingly strong evidence, both statistical and paleontological, that life could *not* have been started on Earth by a series of random chemical reactions. Today's best mathematical estimates state that there simply was not enough time for random reactions to get life going as fast as the fossil record shows that it did. The reactions were either directed by some, as of yet unknown, physical force or a metaphysical guide, or life arrived here from elsewhere. But the 'elsewhere' answer merely pushes the start of life into an even more unlikely time constraint (Dr. Gerald L. Shroeder, *Genesis and the Big Bang,* 25).

"Random reactions," indeed! "Directed by some . . . metaphysical guide." Why not say "God," as in the book of Genesis.

Elizabeth A. Schroeter has remarked on the fallibility of scientific theory and ideas:

> The theory of the evolution of man is based on suppositions and inferences. As an example, the first chapter of Charles Darwin's book, *The Descent of Man*, contains within a few pages 20 expressions of uncertainty such as "seemed," "it appears," "take for granted," "may," and "implies." The concluding chapter of 14 pages has more than 50 such expressions. Within 30 years after publication the book was changed in 87 places.

Stephen Hawking's book makes reference to God repeatedly. From the outset of the volume, he appears as one who sincerely is attempting a "wedding," though he is not yet a real creationist. He wishes to unite the bride and groom; science and religion. "The newly-won knowledge of the universe is in fact," he declares, "the fertile ground for traditions flowering." So he attempts in his own way to reconcile the discoveries in the fields of physics and mathematics, etc., with the age-long pronouncements of religion in the field of creation. His attempts at reconciliation, while noble and scholarly, leave much to be desired. Why is this? Because only by accepting a literal reading of Genesis 1 can the quest for truth about time and matter, the world and space, humans and their creation be positively understood.

The Creator as Eyewitness

God Himself made the earth, and God still lives. He was more than the active party in creation. He and the angels were obviously eyewitnesses—the only eyewitnesses to creation who live today. His testimony is needed, and it is recorded by Moses in Genesis. A subject as important as time and creation requires that a good God-Creator reveal the facts to the human race. Thus Moses tells us what happened when the earth came forth ex nihilo. Moses' record has no ifs or ands about it. In the book of Genesis, there are no such words as *seemed* or *implies* or *take for granted* or *it appears*. The word of God about creation is certain and sure. He speaks as One having authority "and not as the scribes."

[God's] creative works are just as incomprehensible as his existence.

"Great is the Lord, and greatly to be praised, and his greatness is unsearchable."

"Which doeth great things, past finding out; yea, and wonders without number."

"God thundereth marvelously with his voice. Great things doeth he, which we cannot comprehend" (*Spiritual Gifts,* 3:93).

The Week and the Sabbath

In the beginning, there was a seven-day week. There, as we have said, we have time encapsuled into twenty-four-hour days and into a week of 168 hours.

"The Hebrew word translated day in Genesis 1 is *yom*. When *yom* is accompanied by a definite number, it always means a literal, twenty-four hour day (e.g. Gen. 7:11; Ex. 16:1)—another indication that the Creation account speaks of literal, twenty-four-hour days."

"So we have the seventh-day Sabbath recurring every seventh day. Why? To remind humans in every generation that God created the earth and all that is in it and that "man need not speculate concerning the origin of the earth and of the universe because it was created by an omniscient, omnipotent, omnipresent God who spake and it was done and who commanded and it stood fast" (*Seventh-day Adventists Believe . . .* , 71).

In the first angel's message of Revelation 14:6, 7, the Creator-God calls upon the whole world—standing on the brink of eternity—to worship "him that made heaven, and earth" (see also verses 9-12). The Lord God invites all to observe the downtrodden seventh-day Sabbath, engraved by the finger of God in the heart and on tables of stone of His Ten Commandments. This is God's call to the last generation of humanity. Will we respond?

"God established the seventh-day Sabbath so that we would

have a weekly reminder that we are creatures of His making. The Sabbath was a gift of grace, speaking not of what we did, but of what God has done. He especially blessed this day and sanctified it so that we would never forget that, besides work, life should include communion with the Creator, rest, and celebration of God's marvelous creative works (Gen. 2:2, 3). To emphasize its importance, the Creator placed the injunction to remember this sacred memorial of His creative power in the center of the moral law as an everlasting sign and symbol of Creation (Ex. 20:8-11; 31:13-17; Eze. 20:20)" (*Seventh-day Adventists Believe . . .*, 74).

Illuminated by the Spirit of God

To the secular mind, the Bible story of Creation and redemption through Jesus Christ is foolishness (see 1 Corinthians 1:17-21; 2:10-16). To the mind illuminated by the Spirit of God, it is received humbly as the one certain truth on the matter.

When He was upon earth, Jesus Christ expressed His belief in the Creation story as recorded by Moses. He certainly knew what He was talking about because He himself was the Creator-God, active in creation. Wrote the apostle John, "In the beginning was the Word, and the Word was with God, and the Word was God. The same was in the beginning with God. All things were made by him; and without him was not anything made that was made. . . . And the Word was made flesh, and dwelt among us, (and we beheld his glory, the glory as of the only begotten of the Father,) full of grace and truth" (John 1:1-3, 14).

Jesus believed in the Creation story. Speaking to the Pharisees, He said, "He . . . made them at the beginning . . . male and female. . . . What therefore God hath joined together, let no man put asunder" (Matthew 19:4, 6). The apostle Paul in Hebrews 1:10 quotes the words of God the Father to His Son, "Thou, Lord, in the beginning hast laid the foundation of the earth." He who is called "the Word" is indeed God the Father's thoughts made audible. In creation He is God the Father's power made visible. The written Word is God's voice speaking almost audibly to men and women, saying, "This is the way, walk ye in it. This is the truth, believe it."

> He who has a knowledge of God and His word has a settled faith in the divinity of the Holy Scriptures. He does not test the Bible by man's ideas of science. He brings these ideas to the test of the unerring standard. He knows that God's word is truth, and truth can never contradict itself; whatever in the teaching of so-called science contradicts the truth of God's revelation is mere human guesswork (*Testimonies for the Church*, 8:325).

" 'In the beginning God created the heaven and the earth' Gen.1:1. In that simple statement we have the Bible declaration of the origin of the material universe; and it is one in which faith finds a reasonable foundation" (*Analyzed Bible*, 1:10).

Sustaining Power of God

That same creative energy exercised by Jesus Christ in the Creation of this world and people—males and females—is daily exercised in sustaining life on this world—all life, flora, and fauna. There is no inherent power in the earth or in the universe by which all things remain alive, by which movement and existence is possible. God the Creator preserves and sustains them. He "covers the heavens with clouds," "prepares rain for the earth," and "makes grass to grow on the mountains. He gives to the beast its food, and to the young ravens that cry" (Psalm 147:8, 9, NKJV; see also Job 26:7-14). He upholds all things by His power, and "in Him all things consist" (Colossians 1:17, NKJV; see also Hebrews 1:3).

What would we do without God? We're dependent upon Him for the function of every cell of our bodies. Every breath, every heartbeat, every blink of the eye speaks of the care of a loving Creator. "In Him we live and move and have our being" (Acts 17:28, NKJV).

But that's not all. Creative power, as exercised in creation, is also active in the miracle of spiritual rebirth.

> God's creative power is involved not only in creation,

but in redemption and restoration. God re-creates hearts (Isa. 44:21-28; Ps. 51:10). "We are His workmanship," Paul said, "created in Christ Jesus for good works" (Eph. 2:10). "If anyone is in Christ, he is a new creation" (2 Cor. 5:17). God, who hurled the many galaxies across the cosmos, uses that same power to re-create the most degraded sinner into His own image.

This redeeming, restoring power is not limited to changing human lives. The same power that originally created the heavens and the earth will, after the final judgment, re-create them—make of them a new and magnificent creation, a new heavens and a new earth (Isa. 65:17-19; Rev. 21:22) (*Seventh-day Adventists Believe . . .* , 76).

The healing of a wound, the restoring of health to the sick, requires the life-giving restorative and creative energy of God (see *Ministry of Healing*, 77). In Jesus Christ, creation and salvation and healing meet and embrace each other. The event of Creation resulted in a majestic and beautiful earth spread abroad with the creatures of God's loving thought and care.

Years ago, a Quaker missionary entertained a wise old Indian chief in his home in New England. "Let me tell you about the best rule by which to live," said the Quaker.

"You must let me decide that question," said the wise old chief, "but tell me, what is that rule?"

The missionary said, "We call it the golden rule: 'Therefore all things whatsoever ye would that men should do to you, do ye even so to them.' "

The Native American rose to his feet and walked back and forth for at least three or four minutes, then sat down and exclaimed, "It is impossible! There is no man who can fulfill this rule unless," and then he paused and said, "unless the Great Spirit should create in him a clean and a new heart. Then it might be possible, only then."

The Indian chief had penetrated the truth of creation. God made the world; He made humans upon the world; He is able to re-create fallen humanity into His own moral image.

The authors of the book *Seventh-day Adventists Believe . . .*

make this mind-tingling observation:

> Both the contrasts and the parallels between Creation and salvation are significant. . . . At Creation Christ commanded, and it was instantly accomplished. Rather than vast periods of metamorphosis, His powerful word was responsible for Creation. In six days He created all. Yet why did it take even six days? Could not He have spoken just once and brought everything into existence in a moment?
>
> Perhaps He took delight in the unfolding of our planet in those six days. Or perhaps this "extended" time has more to do with the value He placed on each created thing or with His desire to reveal the seven-day week as a model for the cycle of activity and rest He intended for man.
>
> But Christ does not just speak salvation into existence. The process of saving people stretches over millenniums. It involves the old and new covenants, Christ's 33 1/2 years on earth and His nearly 2,000 years of subsequent heavenly intercession. Here is a vast span of time—according to Scripture chronology, about 6,000 years since Creation—and people still have not been returned to the Garden of Eden (76, 77).

Antediluvian Giants

Speaking of persons who lived just before the Flood but long after Creation week, Moses wrote, "There were giants in the earth in those days; and also after that, when the sons of God came in unto the daughters of men, and they bare children to them, the same became mighty men which were of old, men of renown" (Genesis 6:4).

And long after the Flood, the earth, in places, could boast people of great stature, the sons of Anak, for example, who dwelt in the south of Canaan. The two spies who returned from their 40-day searching out of the land testified, "There we saw the giants, the sons of Anak, which come of the giants: and we were in our own sight as grasshoppers, and so we were in their sight" (Numbers 13:33). Real Goliaths!

Adam and Eve were of giant size, nearly twice as large as the average human today. Weight measures logarithmically as size increases. Accordingly, they must have been eight hundred pounds or more. Eve was shorter than Adam, beautifully formed and loveliest of all God's creation.

Degeneration, rather than progression, is the testimony of the earth's creatures. The life of a human being itself teaches us that. There is a time in our existence when nature is building us up all the time. Then there is the stage when decline, loss of energy, the inroads of disease, and old age take place. Why is there this transition from a building-up process to a degenerative process? Certainly this never would have existed in Adam and Eve had they not sinned, because with sin came degeneration and death. This points up the vital truth that the fall of humankind as recorded in Scripture is to be blamed for the degenerative processes in the living creation.

On the other hand, evolution teaches progression, but the facts of life itself, whether the flora, the fauna, or human life, inform us pathetically that there is no progression; we only live and die. The transition of one form into another form, of one species into another species, that is, the missing link, is still the great conundrum of evolutionary scientists. Where is the convincing paleontological evidence that the species has changed? The names arbitrarily attached to skeletons, or parts of skeletons, project links in a man-made theory but not coercive evidence.

Discover a Complete Theory?

Steven Hawking is considered by many the most brilliant theoretical physicist since Einstein, and his book confronts the question of the nature of time in the universe. Was there a beginning of time? Will there be an end? Is the universe infinite, or does it have boundaries? When confronting these overwhelming issues, like many scientists he must theorize because he does not have the infallible Book to guide him.

Hawking asks the question, "Why does the universe go to all the bother of existing? Is the unified theory so compelling that it brings about its own existence? Or does it need a creator, and, if so, does he have any other effect on the universe? And who created him?" (*A Brief History of Time*, 174).

He concludes his book by saying, "If we do discover a complete theory, it should in time be understandable in broad principle by everyone, not just a few scientists. Then we shall all, philosophers, scientists and just ordinary people, be able to take part in the discussion of the question of why it is that we and the universe exist. If we find the answer to that, it would be the ultimate triumph of human reason—for then we would know the mind of God" (ibid., 175).

But we do know the mind of God and the reason why the universe exists. Listen to the prophet Isaiah: "Thus saith the Lord that created the heavens; God himself that formed the earth and made it; he hath established it, *he created it not in vain, he formed it to be inhabited*: I am the Lord; and there is none else" (Isaiah 45:18, emphasis added).

Again, John the apostle informs us: "Thou art worthy, O Lord, to receive glory and honour and power: for *thou hast created all things, and for thy pleasure they are and were created*" (Revelation 4:11, emphasis added).

Do we know the mind of God? Not in everything, but in all essential things! God delights in sharing His life and truth with rational creatures. It brought great pleasure to Him to make Adam and Eve in the beginning. It brought enormous pleasure to Him to make Adam and Eve procreators with Himself—to be able to reproduce and have children of their own. Indeed, from their posterity came the Saviour of the world, the Son of God, who came into the world to teach humanity what God is like, to show something of His love and wisdom and power, and to reenact by His miracles the creative work of God.

Chapter 5:

Exodus 20

GOD'S TEN IMMORTAL WORDS

Let's start this chapter with just a few relevant questions: What moral code comes closest to a worldwide, all-embracing standard for right and wrong? What is the universal yardstick by which human behavior and divine-human relationships can be accurately measured? Is there such a measuring device available to human beings, to the church and the state, as well as the individual, the family, and the community; to the judge and jury in a criminal trial for manslaughter; to a city court in a civil trial for a misdemeanor? Has God provided a dependable device to show what's good and what's bad?

Do we derive moral guidance intuitively or instinctively? Is the conscience of man a safe guide? Maybe the expression "natural law" explains it. Paul observes that

> when Gentiles who have not [the divine] Law do instinctively what the Law requires, they are a law to themselves, since they do not have the Law. They show that the essential requirements of the Law are written in their hearts and are operating there; with which their conscience (sense of right and wrong) also bears witness; and their [moral] decisions—their arguments of reason, their condemning or approving thoughts—will accuse or perhaps defend and excuse [them] (Romans 2:14, 15, Amplified Bible, 225, 226).

Through the centuries, Christian boards and tribunals have

47

had the help they needed to tell the difference between true and false worship; to develop male and female relationships; to identify idolatry and the nature of irreverence and blasphemy and violence; to distinguish between honesty and dishonesty; and to understand why men and women behave the way they do.

Something more definitive than conscience, instinct, or intuitiveness is a necessity. Is there some age-old writing inscribed on parchment or stone that settles the difference between right and wrong, good and evil? If the Almighty has a government, a kingdom, there has got to be a law!

The answer is as clear as the sky on that dark night over Mount Sinai when brilliant flashes of light from God's glorious presence burst forth and from His lips pealed out in thunder tones the immortal words of the Ten Commandments. It was a supercolossal event, the greatest in all judicial history. The record appeared on two stone tablets. The date was about 1500 B.C.

Christ Proclaims the Law

So that we can understand fully that these laws represented a good God's very nature and that they were good laws, God sent His Son, Jesus Christ, to earth to interpret the moral law by the perfect life He lived and the sacrificial death He died. Indeed, it was He, the immortal Christ, who proclaimed the law at Sinai, the Father standing by His side.

When the law was spoken, the Lord, the Creator of heaven and earth, stood by the side of His Son, enshrouded in the fire and the smoke on the mount. It was not here that the law was first given; but it was proclaimed, that the children of Israel, whose ideas had become confused in their association with idolaters in Egypt, might be reminded of its terms, and understand what constitutes the true worship of Jehovah (Ellen G. White Comments, *SDA Bible Commentary*, 1:1103, 1104).

Love in the Law

But the law as proclaimed on Mount Sinai was not so much

prohibition against evil practices as promises to be mightily preserved from evil.

That law of ten precepts of the greatest love that can be presented to man is the voice of God from heaven speaking to the soul in promise, "This do, and you will not come under the dominion and control of Satan." There is not a negative in that law, although it may appear thus. It is DO, and Live (*SDA Bible Commentary,* 1:1105).

Love for God and humanity summarizes the moral law. The law of Jehovah dating back to Creation, was comprised in two great principles: "Thou shalt love the Lord thy God with all thy heart, and with all thy soul, and with all thy mind, and with all thy strength: this is the first commandment. And the second is like, namely this, Thou shalt love thy neighbour as thyself. There is none other commandment greater than these" (Mark 12:30, 31). These two great principles embrace the first four commandments, written by the finger of God Himself on the first tablet, showing the duty of humans to God, and the last six, showing the duty of humans to their neighbors, on the second tablet of stone. Christ is the Rock—His law, written in stone, is as enduring as He is.

While love can be defined (see 1 Corinthians 13), it does not particularize its own behavior. The Ten Commandments do. Love behaves according to the ten Words of God.

Only the principles found in God's written code of life provide the wisdom needed to make right choices and the love motivation demanded for success. God Himself is represented by His law, and the man, woman, or child who is guided by these precepts will have grace from God to be and to do right. And at this point of obedience to God's law, we face an enormous moral and theological conundrum! Law keeping by fallen humanity, disjointed and rebellious, is said to be an impossibility. But is it? Jesus, the divine Lord, was also a human being. Think about this.

Have you ever heard the saying, "Rules were made to be broken!" Is this right or wrong? Legislative bodies produce laws that were meant to be kept, not violated, but there are always some violators. God's Ten Commandment laws were also meant to be kept, but every man, woman, and child who has lived on earth, except Jesus, has been a transgressor of this holy law. But the law of God was not made to be broken.

The glory of the gospel is that divine grace provides, through the "nonviolator" Jesus Christ, the power to become obedient sons and daughters of God. John 1:12 says, "As many as received him, to them gave he power to become the sons of God, even to them that believe on his name."

Nietzsche, the German philosopher, remarked, "If you expect me to believe in the Redeemer, you Christians must act as if you are redeemed."

But before obedience is possible, it is necessary to identify with Jesus, the Lawgiver, by faith. He is both Lawgiver and Saviour of Israel. He appeared to Moses in the burning bush, commissioning the eighty-year-old shepherd to appear before Pharaoh demanding the release of the hostage Israelites (see Exodus 3:13-15). Who commanded Moses? Jesus testified that it was He Himself, the great "I AM." To the Jews of His time, Jesus said, "Your father Abraham rejoiced to see my day: and he saw it, and was glad. Then said the Jews unto him, Thou art not yet fifty years old, and hast thou seen Abraham? Jesus said unto them, Verily, verily, I say unto you, Before Abraham was, I am" (John 8:56-58; see also 1 Corinthians 10:1-4).

"I am the Lord thy God" (Exodus 20:2). Jesus is the great I AM, the self-existent One, whose life has neither beginning nor ending. It was He who opened up the Red Sea, who turned the bitter waters into sweet, who brought forth water from the rock, who appeared on Mount Sinai and gave the law of God. He is the bread of life, light of the world, door to the sheepfold, Shepherd. Jesus is all of this and more!

Obedience to the commandments of God requires a miracle, as much a miracle as opening up the Red Sea to the Hebrews, as bringing the water from the rock, and as healing the bitter waters and making them sweet. This miracle Christ accomplishes in all who accept Him and His way of life as the way of salvation.

Observe how this salvation functions: "I am the Lord thy God"—Christ identifies Himself to Israel at Mount Sinai— "which have brought thee out of the land of Egypt, out of the house of bondage"—He declares Himself the Lord of emancipation—"As I miraculously made the exodus from Egypt a historical reality and witness, so I will miraculously make your lives a history of victory from:

1. Polytheism
2. Idolatry and false worship
3. Profanity and irreverence
4. Disobedience (Sabbath breaking)
5. Contempt of authority
6. Criminal violence
7. Adultery and fornication
8. Theft and robbery
9. Falsehood
10. Covetousness."

These Ten Commandments are ten promises of what God can do to transform the loyal and believing soul into a human with the divine nature, or character (see 2 Peter 1:4). Think of how this law was observed in the life of Christ as a human being.

1. In His humanity, except for His Father, God, He worshiped no deity, no object or thing or person, but how ardent was His worship of the Father in heaven!

2. In His humanity, He gave no consent to image worship, and He erected no shrine. To the tempter in the wilderness, He declared, "Thou shalt worship the Lord thy God, and him only shalt thou serve" (Matthew 4:10).

3. Never once did He disgrace or profane the name of His Father, but He honored the name of the Father. He drove from the temple those who made the sacred dwelling place a den of thieves.

4. He was the interpreter of correct Sabbath keeping and declared Himself to be "the Lord of the Sabbath." He upset and demolished the legalistic restrictions of the fanatical scribes and Pharisees, who added burdens that need not be borne. It is lawful to do good on the Sabbath day, He declared.

5. He honored His mother by committing her to the care of

John while He was dying on the cross. Precious Saviour! How love shone through in His last unselfish act of caring!

6. Stealing was contrary to His character. He was a Giver, bestowing bread upon the hungry multitude and life upon the sick and dying.

7. He was single and unmarried, unfamiliar with the practice of sex in any form, but He declared through Paul that marriage is honorable and the bed undefiled. It was adultery He spurned. He bade the woman taken in this sin to go and sin no more. He was against sexual sinning.

8. Murder. He blamed the devil for it and declared that he was the father and originator of it. As the Lifegiver, He raised the dead, and being the victim of murderous men Himself, He came forth from the grave with life that was in Himself.

9. His enemies might lie, but He would not and could not lie, for He said, "I am the way, the truth, and the life," while Satan was a liar from the beginning and the father of lies.

10. What was it that He coveted? Nothing more than the favor and blessing of God upon a world infected by discontent and evil.

He did not lust after His neighbor's wife nor anything that was His neighbor's. He desired only His neighbor's good.

Christ "is a perfect and holy example, given for us to imitate. We cannot equal the pattern; but we shall not be approved of God if we do not copy it and, according to the ability which God has given, resemble it" (*Testimonies for the Church,* 2:549).

If Any Man Sin—?

And if anyone sins after experiencing God's grace, what then?

> My little children, these things write I unto you, that ye sin not. And if any man sin, we have an advocate with the Father, Jesus Christ the righteous: and he is the propitiation for our sins: and not for our's [sic] only, but also for the sins of the whole world. And hereby we do know that we know him, if we keep his commandments. He that saith, I know him, and keepeth not his commandments, is a liar, and the truth is not in him. But whoso keepeth his word,

in him verily is the love of God perfected: hereby know we that we are in him. He that saith he abideth in him ought himself also so to walk, even as he walked (1 John 2:1-6).

What do Seventh-day Adventists believe about this?

Seventh-day Adventists believe the great principles of God's law are embodied in the Ten Commandments and exemplified in the life of Christ. They express God's love, will, and purposes concerning human conduct and relationships and are binding upon all people in every age. These precepts are the basis of God's covenant with His people and the standard in God's judgment. Through the agency of the Holy Spirit they point out sin and awaken a sense of need for a Saviour. Salvation is all of grace and not of works, but its fruitage is obedience to the Commandments. This obedience develops Christian character and results in a sense of well-being. It is an evidence of our love for the Lord and our concern for our fellow men. The obedience of faith demonstrates the power of Christ to transform lives, and therefore strengthens Christian witness *(Seventh-day Adventist Believe . . . , 232).*

The Law—Burden or Delight?

Is the law of God a chore to observe, a burden to the soul? Listen to the psalmist: "Oh, how I love Your law! It is my meditation all the day." "I love Your commandments more than gold, yes, than fine gold!" Even when "trouble and anguish have overtaken me," he said, "Your commandments are my delights" (Psalm 119:97, 127, 143, NKJV). To those who love God, "His commandments are not burdensome" (1 John 5:3, NKJV). Transgressors are the ones who consider the law a grievous yoke, for the sinful mind "does not submit to God's law, nor can it do so" (Romans 8:7, NIV).

The law functions like a mirror (see James 1:23-25). Those who "look" into it see their own character defects in contrast to God's righteous character. So the moral law demonstrates that all the world is guilty before God (Romans 3:19). The gospel invites all the world to seek forgiveness in Christ, who tasted death for every person.

"When the editor of a small newspaper was short of material to fill his columns one week, he asked his typesetter to fill in with the Ten Commandments. After that week's issue had been circulated, the editor received a letter from one reader saying, 'Cancel my subscription. You are getting too personal' " (*Sourcebook for Speakers*, 350). Indeed, the law does get "personal," probing a person's very motives and behavior. In Jesus' Sermon on the Mount, He magnified the law and X-rayed the commandments one by one, teaching that transgression begins inside and works its way out (see Matthew 5:17-48). And the law is the standard in the final judgment of the God of all the earth (Ecclesiastes 12:13, 14; James 2:8-13). And Jesus will be the Judge as well as Advocate (see John 5:22-27; 1 Timothy 2:5, 6).

Final Conflict Over the Law

Bible prophecy emphasizes that the devil will attack the law of God and His church (see Revelation 12) and a commandment-keeping church will rise in its defense. There will be a battle to the death—a final conflict (see Revelation 13).

Here is Ellen White's prophetic view of the future conflict and the ultimate triumph, a masterpiece of symbolic representation:

In vision I saw two armies in terrible conflict. One army was led by banners bearing the world's insignia; the other was led by the bloodstained banner of Prince Immanuel. Standard after standard was left to trail in the dust as company after company from the Lord's army joined the foe and tribe after tribe from the ranks of the enemy united with the commandment-keeping people of God. An angel flying in the midst of heaven put the standard of Immanuel into many hands, while a mighty general cried out with a loud voice: "Come into line. Let those who are loyal to the commandments of God and the testimony of Christ now take their position. Come out from among them, and be ye separate, and touch not the unclean, and I will receive you, and will be a Father unto you, and ye shall be My sons and daughters. Let all who will come up to the help of the Lord, to the help of the Lord against the mighty."

The battle raged. Victory alternated from side to side. Now the soldiers of the cross gave way, "as when a standardbearer fainteth." Isaiah 10:18. But their apparent retreat was but to gain a more advantageous position. Shouts of joy were heard. A song of praise to God went up, and angel voices united in the song, as Christ's soldiers planted His banner on the walls of fortresses till then held by the enemy. The Captain of our salvation was ordering the battle and sending support to His soldiers. His power was mightily displayed, encouraging them to press the battle to the gates. He taught them terrible things in righteousness as He led them on step by step, conquering and to conquer.

At last the victory was gained. The army following the banner with the inscription, "The commandments of God, and the faith of Jesus," was gloriously triumphant. The soldiers of Christ were close beside the gates of the city, and with joy the city received her King. The kingdom of peace and joy and everlasting righteousness was established (*Testimonies for the Church*, 8:41, 42).

Triumph, yes, but how? Can men and women be saved eternally by keeping the law? No. As a method of salvation, law keeping is impossible and fruitless. Obedience for obedience' sake is not profitable, but God requires obedience to the law. This we cannot render. By the miracle of the Spirit's working, born-again Christians are transformed into law abiding citizens of the kingdom of God. Jesus, in His sinless humanity, rendered obedience to the law, and for those who by faith accept Him as Lord and Saviour, His perfect obedience to the moral law is counted as righteousness and imputed, put to the account of the believing sinner. It becomes also a tangible reality in daily obedience, through the power of the Spirit of God.

There is therefore now no condemnation to them which are in Christ Jesus, who walk not after the flesh, but after the Spirit. For the law of the Spirit of life in Christ Jesus hath made me free from the law of sin and death. For what the law could not do, in that it was weak through the flesh, God sending his own Son in the likeness of sinful flesh, and for sin, condemned sin in the flesh: that the righteousness of the law might be fulfilled in us, who walk not after the flesh, but after the Spirit (Romans 8:1-4).

Satan had claimed that it was impossible for man to obey God's commandments; and in our own strength it is true that we cannot obey them. But Christ came in the form of humanity, and by His perfect obedience He proved that humanity and divinity combined can obey every one of God's precepts.

'As many as received Him, to them gave He power to become the sons of God, even to them that believe on His name." John 1:12. This power is not in the human agent. It is the power of God. When a soul receives Christ, he receives power to live the life of Christ' (*Christ's Object Lessons*, 314).

"Christ," Paul says, "is the end of the law for righteousness to everyone who believes" (Romans 10:4); that is, those who believe in Christ as Saviour and Lord know that He puts an end to law keeping as a way of obtaining righteousness. No longer do they count on law keeping, or doing good, to find favor with God. Now at last, the new life of obedience and right doing springs from a new creation of God—the new person born of the Spirit of God.

Chapter 6:

Matthew 5

THE GREATEST SERMON

There is no evidence that Jesus ever spoke from a prepared text. He had no sermon notes. God taught Him what to say, and as He came forth from His study and prayer, the Holy Spirit spoke through the inspired language.

As something strange and new, these words [The Beatitudes] fall upon the ears of the wondering multitude. Such teaching is contrary to all they have ever heard from priest or rabbi. They see in it nothing to flatter their pride or to feed their ambitious hopes. But there is about this new Teacher a power that holds them spellbound. The sweetness of divine love flows from His very presence as the fragrance from a flower. His words fall like "rain upon the mown grass: as showers that water the earth." Psalm 72:6. All feel instinctively that here is One who reads the secrets of the soul, yet who comes near to them with tender compassion. Their hearts open to Him, and, as they listen, the Holy Spirit unfolds to them something of the meaning of that lesson which humanity in all ages so needs to learn (*Thoughts From the Mount of Blessing*, 6).

Jesus' immortal discourse captures the mind, heart, and imagination. It begins with a prologue found in verses 1 and 2. Following that is what one writer calls "the full manifesto" in 5:3–7:27. The epilogue is presented in Matthew 7:28, 29.

57

It's too bad that sermons are sometimes regarded contemptuously. Not so Jesus' Sermon on the Mount. Let us take the first segment, Matthew chapter 5, and in imagination join the crowd as they open their hearts to the greatest single discourse ever presented in the six millenniums of human history.

The occasion for the sermon is revealed in the statement about Jesus' "seeing the multitudes" (Matthew 5:1). Who were these people? From what classes of society did they come, and why were they attracted to Jesus? In a sweeping statement found in chapter 4:23-25, Matthew testifies concerning the crowds that followed Jesus:

> Jesus went about all Galilee, teaching in their synagogues, and preaching the gospel of the kingdom, and healing all manner of sickness and all manner of disease among the people. And his fame went throughout all Syria: and they brought unto him all sick people that were taken with divers diseases and torments, and those which were possessed with devils, and those which were lunatick, and those that had the palsy; and he healed them. And there followed him great multitudes of people from Galilee, and from Decapolis, and from Jerusalem, and from Judaea, and from beyond Jordan.

And so the "multitudes" gather about Him on the mount. The lunatics come to hear Him, not only on the mount but on other occasions. After He teaches, He heals. They leave sane and in their right minds. The lepers come to hear Him. They depart clean and completely restored. The devil-possessed, freshly emancipated from demonic control, cannot wait to tell what Jesus has done for them. The palsied and crippled, with newly found strength of limb and nerve, rejoice with a joy that is unspeakable. The young and the old, the scribes, the priests, the Sadducees, the Pharisees, the soldiers, and all the curious caught up in the multitude to hear Jesus are spellbound!

> The Prince of heaven was among His people. The greatest gift of God had been given to the world. Joy to the poor;

for Christ had come to make them heirs of His kingdom. Joy to the rich; for He would teach them how to secure eternal riches. Joy to the ignorant; He would make them wise unto salvation. Joy to the learned; He would open to them deeper mysteries than they had ever fathomed; truths that had been hidden from the foundation of the world would be opened to men by the Saviour's mission (*The Desire of Ages*, 277).

Jesus' message on the mount was intended, first, for the disciples for they were the future leaders of the church and needed more than anyone else in the huge crowd to understand the principles governing the kingdom of His grace. These principles were presented by the great Teacher to govern all of human life. Human problems can never be solved while ignoring His instructions. There can never be maturity of spiritual life in any of us if these matters are neglected.

The Octave of Beatitudes

At the very outset of this "class instruction," the Master Teacher presented the "octave of beatitudes"—seven plus one! The perfect number plus one, for good measure.

The King enunciated the principles and the laws of the Kingdom of God. He struck the keynote of the Divine thought and purpose in the very first word that fell from His lips, "Blessed." That is the purpose of God for humanity. One might, with perfect accuracy, render that word, "happy." As a matter of fact, taking the two words, "blessed" and "happy," as we use them to-day, both values are found in the word which our Lord employed (G. Campbell Morgan, *Great Chapters of the Bible*, 119, 120).

Who are the blessed? The answer Christ gave represents the positive principles that appeared in His own life and ministry. He is the Blessed One! Note that all of the qualities of people upon whom He bestowed blessings appeared in His personal life: (1) *humility and meekness* (Matthew 8:18-20); (2) *sorrow-*

ing; Jesus was "a man of sorrows, and acquainted with grief (Isaiah 53:3). (3) *meekness* (Matthew 8:18-20); (4) *seeking after righteousness* (Psalm 40:7-10); (5) *mercy and compassion* (Matthew 4:23, 24; 9:36); (6) *pureness of heart* (Hebrews 7:26); (7) *peacemaking* (John 14:27); (8) *enduring persecution* (John 10:23-27; Matthew 10:22-26).

What is Jesus saying here? Blessed are the Christlike. Happy are those who seek to be like the King, to imitate Him, who are changed from the old life of sinning to the new life of imitating and copying the Saviour.

A New Life for the Old

Soon after Pentecost, Peter preached in the temple to a multitude of Jews, many of whom had just witnessed the remarkable healing of the cripple at the Gate Beautiful. He testified to them, "Unto you first God, having raised up his Son Jesus, sent him to *bless you*, in turning away every one of you from his iniquities" (Acts 3:26, emphasis added).

Peter explains that Jesus was sent "to bless you." Of what did the blessing consist? "Turning away every one of you from his iniquities." So a blessing administered by Jesus consists, among other things, of a saving act—many saving acts—emancipation from sinful habits, a new life altogether. It is much more than a "bless you" pronounced over one who sneezes or a good night benediction to one's spouse. The stock in trade of the Master Teacher Jesus was to deliver a new life for the old, to proclaim liberty to the captives of sin.

The Beatitudes identify in adjective form—*blessed*—the character of the people who win heaven at last, while *to bless you* a verb form, tells of Jesus' action on the human heart, through the Holy Spirit, transforming the believing sinner into the image of God. So the people who are blessed have been turned away from their iniquities to a new life through faith in God.

Like Salt and Light

In verses 13-16, Jesus further describes "the kingdom people." They are like salt, with the purpose of providing flavor to society. A vital, living presence acts as a leaven to illustrate the divine character lived out in human experience; it is a power to remove forever the charge against God that no role models exist to show how divine power can transform believing people and through them teach the world how to live. Unfortunately, many who profess religion are like salt that has lost its savor—they "become insipid."

It would be as unthinkable for a Christian to lose his essential characteristics and still be a Christian as it would be for salt to lose its saltiness and still be considered and used as salt. If Christians are such in name only, their nominal citizenship in the kingdom of heaven becomes a farce. They are not Christians unless they reflect the character of Christ, regardless of what their profession may be (*SDA Bible Commentary*, 5:330).

Then there is the light—it stands out as distinct from darkness as fresh salt is different from salt that has lost its savor. No more fireflies, Jesus is saying, but illumination like a city standing forth on a hill, like a lamp on a table in a darkened room. And how does the light reveal itself? By "your good works." You are to show forth the explosive quality of the new affection you have gained. Christians don't just talk! They "perform the doing of it," as Paul says in 2 Corinthians 8:11.

It's possible that James, Jesus' elder brother—by Joseph through a former marriage—may have been there to listen that day, and how was he impressed? Hear these words:

What doth it profit, my brethren, though a man say he hath faith, and have not works? can faith save him? If a brother or sister be naked, and destitute of daily food, and one of you say unto them, Depart in peace, be ye warmed and filled; notwithstanding ye give them not those things which are needful to the body; what doth it profit? Even so faith, if it hath not works, is dead, being alone. Yea, a man may say, Thou hast faith, and I have works: shew me thy faith without thy works, and I will shew thee my faith by my works (James 2:14-18).

Salt is chemically identified by four letters: *NACL*. It is a preservative. Light appears as a treasury of colors when it passes through a triangular prism; more scientifically, it is a form of electromagnetic radiation that acts on the retina of the eye, making sight possible. Spiritually, it is a Person who says concerning Himself, "I am the light of the world" (John 8:12), and to His followers, "Ye are the light of the world" (Matthew 5:14). When Jesus came, there was no light. When He left, there was no darkness. Have you ever thought that in darkness there is no choice, but when there is light we can see the difference between things of earth and heaven. And it is Christ who provides this light! And as Christians, we are to supply this light to all the world. As a result, multitudes will decide between light and darkness and be saved (see Joel 3:14).

Christians are like rainbows that stand out against dark clouds and give promise of new life; they are like fires that burn and glow and give off heat with every bright ray. Jesus, the Son of Righteousness, conveys power and energy to every soul exposed to His presence and makes them glow and go for God! So, in a larger sense, the church is to be radiant with the light that glows from a myriad of candles. The people who accept His teaching and receive Him into their hearts are transformed, forgiven and accepted by God. They are now a part of the kingdom of grace. Not only are they light bearers, but they are law keepers, as we shall see.

The Divine Law Magnified

In Matthew 5:17-47, Jesus turns the microscope of divine wisdom on the second table of the law. In verses 21-32 He magnifies the divine statutes prohibiting murder and adultery.

Jesus lived as a single. He was unmarried. He was also about thirty years old when He preached this sermon. His life was an overflow of divine love for all people. The purity of His life was pristine and glorified. The commandments He gave were aimed at eliminating murder and adultery.

"Whosoever shall say, Thou fool" or "whoever calls down curses upon him" (Today's Christian New Testament)—this is a preliminary to striking a blow with a club or stabbing with a knife or the shooting a pistol or putting poison in the cup. Murder is stamped on each preliminary move. The commandment is violated before the physical act itself.

By the same token, "whosoever looketh on a woman to lust after her hath committed adultery with her already in his heart" (Matthew 5:28). The first look at an attractive woman or a handsome man is innocent enough. We may see such people every day in the office, on the streets, at church, at an entertainment. To recognize that a person is beautiful or handsome is doing no wrong. But the second look could be a serpentine of fire that springs from the passion lurking in the body. James tells us that "every man is tempted, when he is drawn away of his own lust, and enticed. Then when lust hath conceived, it bringeth forth sin: and sin, when it is finished, bringeth forth death" (James 1:14, 15).

Lust is prologue to the physical act, preliminary to the sensuous encounter in the bedroom. Jesus made plain that sin must be nipped in the bud, stopped before it starts. That's the kind of life He lived. He wanted us to be like Him, pure minded and lovingly disposed to every man, woman, and child. Let the man with stars in his eyes respect every lovely lady and not expect to receive sexual favors from her. And when the lovely lady sees the stars in his eyes, let her calm his desires by her modest behavior!

In Scripture, homosexuality and lesbianism are frowned upon (see Romans 1:26-28, 32). In his basic New Testament teaching, the apostle Paul could boast of his Corinthian brethren, many of whom had experienced adultery or homosexual perversion (Romans 1:9, NEB). "Such were some of you," said the apostle Paul. For the Romans, being a Christian meant being obedient to natural law. Conversion cured perversion! But with some who are addicted to the practice, it is slow going. God does not give them up, nor should we.

Child abuse is common today; in fact, the sordid picture of today's society is not complete unless we mention a report about children ten or twelve years of age forcing five- or six-year-old children to perform sexual acts. The teachings of Jesus, if accepted and practiced, would prevent all of these ugly encounters.

Now, how do we explain Jesus' teaching about putting away one's wife?

"Putting away" was common among the Jews. The law of Moses permitted a husband to put away his wife for any reason whatsoever, but Jesus cared about women divorced by selfish husbands, and He indicated that no husband had a right to put away his wife unless she had been unfaithful to him. He then declared that the man who married the divorced woman committed adultery; that is, a woman who was put away for fornication and married another caused that man to commit adultery. On the other hand, if the husband had maintained an adulterous relationship with another woman and put away his innocent wife, she was free to marry again, but only one who was "in the Lord."

The Commandments Are Eternal

Consider the following:

Since "the law of the Lord is perfect," every variation from it must be evil. Those who disobey the commandments of God, and teach others to do so, are reproved by Christ. The Saviour's life of obedience maintained the claims of the law; it proved that the law could be kept in humanity, and showed the excellence of character that obedience would develop. All who obey as He did are likewise declaring that the law is "holy, and just, and good." Rom. 7:12. On the other hand, all who break God's commandments are sustaining Satan's claim that the law is unjust, and cannot be obeyed. Thus they second the deceptions of the great adversary, and cast dishonor upon God. They are the children of the wicked one, who was the first rebel against God's law. To admit them into heaven would again bring in the elements of discord and rebellion, and imperil the well-being of the universe. No man who willfully disregards one principle of the law shall enter the kingdom of heaven (*The Desire of Ages*, 308, 309).

Three Eternal Principles

Matthew 5, verses 33 to 37, 38 to 42, and 43 to 48 represent three eternal principles.

1. Open-faced, unaffected honesty needs no oath or formal swearing by heaven or earth to support it. A person's word is his bond.

2. Meekness and self-control, not force and violence, are the insignia of God's people in His kingdom.

3. Unselfish, outgoing, second-mile religion is the way to peace and happiness, and the hallmark of Christian maturity and perfection.

Jesus' exemplary life illustrates this trinity of principles in practice:

1. Jesus was as transparent as the sunlight. Why should He ever support what He had to say with an oath? It is true that in Matthew 26:63, 64 He accepted the oath imposed upon Him by Caiaphas. Why? Because the name of God and the sacredness of His own identity were at stake.

"But Jesus kept silent. And the high priest said to Him, I call upon you to swear by the living God, and tell us whether you are the Christ, the Son of God. Jesus said to him, You have stated [the fact]. More than that, I tell you, You will in the future see the Son of man seated at the right hand of the Almighty, and coming on the clouds of the sky" (Matthew 26:63, 64, Amplified Bible).

2. Jesus' behavior at many trials, under duress and the cruelest treatment, was marked by a meekness and self-control that was godlike (See Matthew 26:47-68; 1 Peter 2:20-25).

3. Matthew 5:44 reads: (1) "Love your enemies," (2) "bless them that curse you," (3) "do good to them that hate you, and" (4) "pray for them which despitefully use you, and persecute you."

This is the supreme test of Christian character, but it was no hurdle for Jesus. At the cross He prayed for those who persecuted Him and questioned His Messiahship.

The Saviour made no murmur of complaint. His face remained calm and serene, but great drops of sweat stood upon His brow. There was no pitying hand to wipe the death dew from His face, nor words of sympathy and unchanging fidelity to stay His human heart. While the soldiers were doing their fearful work, Jesus prayed for His enemies, "Father, forgive them; for they know not what they do." His mind passed from His own suffering to the sin of His persecutors, and the terrible retribution that would be theirs. No curses were called down upon the soldiers who were handling Him so roughly. No vengeance was invoked upon the priests and rulers, who were gloating over the accomplishment of their purpose. Christ pitied them in their ignorance and guilt. He breathed only a plea for their forgiveness,—"for they know not what they do." . . .

That prayer of Christ for His enemies embraced the world. It took in every sinner that had lived or should live, from the beginning of the world to the end of time. Upon all rests the guilt of crucifying the Son of God. To all, forgiveness is freely offered. "Whosoever will" may have peace with God, and inherit eternal life (*The Desire of Ages*, 744, 745).

But now this closing and sobering note from the pen of an observing Jew in which he chastises Christians for failing to actually live the Sermon on the Mount: First of all, he refers to Mahatma Gandhi, who wrote: "The message of Jesus, as I understand it, is contained in the Sermon on the Mount. . . . It is that *Sermon* which has endeared Jesus to me." Then this Jewish rabbi declared, "A good many Jews can repeat that statement just as sincerely as they can accept Gandhi's subsequent criticism: 'The message, to my mind, has suffered distortion in the West. . . . Much of what passes as Christianity is a negation of the *Sermon on the Mount*.' "

But truly those who have found grace to imitate Christ have reached a point of Christian maturity akin to Christ and His Father in heaven. We become holy in the human sphere as God is holy in the divine sphere. That is what it means to be "perfect" (Matthew 5:48).

Chapter 7:

2 Peter 1

THE KEYNOTE TO VICTORY

Have you ever observed on TV the super excitement as the winners of the Super Bowl return to their native city to receive honors? I've seen it here in Washington, D.C., twice. It's spectacular. Quarterbacks and receivers are revered. A fullback who carried the ball across the line to help sweep the Redskins to victory was hailed as a god!

The Super Bowl is a hyperthyroid, megacolossal event, with all the stops pulled out. People get supercharged and go crazy. Rejoicing is loud and long. People collect on bets, they wave banners, they throw parties. It's not only a paroxysm of fun, but also big business. It's victory time. It's the ultimate thing!

But the real contests of life—the battles, the wars, the ones that yield eternal prizes—are not fought on gridirons, tennis courts, polished basketball courts, or even on the battlefield. The real game of life—the war, the controversy between Christ and Satan—is fought in the heart of the Christian. "We wrestle not against flesh and blood, but against principalities, against powers, against the rulers of the darkness of this world" (Ephesians 6:12). But not for long. Soon the controversy will end with consummate victory. God Himself, "with the voice of a great thunder" and a multitude of "harpers harping with their harps" while the redeemed burst forth in "a new song," announces to the universe that celebration time has come at last, that the armies of God in heaven and on earth have won the war. Armageddon results in triumph (Revelation 14:2, 3)!

All Things Made Possible

In 2 Peter, chapter 1, the apostle, who had his share of warfare building up the kingdom of God, sounds a glorious *keynote of victory*. In the most inspiring language, he describes how God has made it possible for Christians to win the war with self and Satan and succeed in the struggle and share in the last final hurrah! "All things that pertain unto life and godliness," he declares, are made possible "through the knowledge of him that hath called us to glory and virtue" (verse 3). *All things!* Pretty inclusive, isn't it!

Paul, as well as Peter, was absolutely convinced that where sin abounded, grace much more abounded. Paul declared, "I can do *all things* through Christ which strengtheneth me" (Philippians 4:13, emphasis added). Paul had been converted. "Old things are passed away; behold, *all things* are become new. And all things are of God, who hath reconciled us to himself by Jesus Christ, and hath given to us the ministry of reconciliation" (2 Corinthians 5:17, 18, emphasis added).

How the Victory Is Won

Note carefully and prayerfully the choice promises and assurances of victory provided by the great apostle Peter.

Verse 1: "Precious faith." How is it obtained? "Through the righteousness of God and our Saviour Jesus Christ."

Verse 2: "Grace and peace be multiplied unto you." How are grace and peace obtained? "Through the knowledge of God, and of Jesus our Lord."

Verse 3: "All things that pertain unto life and godliness" are assured. How are they obtained? "Through the knowledge of him that hath called us to glory and virtue."

Verse 4: "Ye might be partakers of the divine nature, having escaped the corruption that is in the world through lust." How do we obtain this divine nature? "Whereby are given unto us exceeding great and precious promises: that by these ye might be partakers of the divine nature, having escaped the corruption that is in the world through lust."

Knowledge gained through reading the "Good News Books"— the four Gospels—is "prime knowledge." To know Jesus is life eternal. The word *know* is found 200 times in the Bible. *Guess* is not found at all! "These things have I written unto you that believe on the name of the Son of God; that ye may know that ye have eternal life, and that ye may believe on the name of the Son of God" (1 John 5:13). That name is Jesus—Saviour. "He is able also to save them to the uttermost that come unto God by him" (Hebrews 7:25).

What God can do! We need to think more about it. We need to realize what the knowledge of Jesus can do.

In old London, Evangeline Booth, daughter of William Booth, founder of the Salvation Army, was leading a soul-winning band—singing, praying, and preaching—in front of a large prison. A group of guards hauled to the gate a screaming, cursing, struggling woman—her hair flying in all directions, a bloodied face, a torn remnant of a dress. "What can I do for that poor soul?" the question raced through Evangeline's mind. Then in a burst of inspiration, she raced over to the gate, embraced the poor woman, and planted a kiss on her scarred face.

All at once the commotion stopped. There was no more struggle, only a question: "Who kissed me?" She repeated the question over and over again.

The next day, when Evangeline had gained permission to visit her, she was still asking, "Who kissed me?" It was a golden opportunity to speak about Jesus and His love and grace. "I kissed you, dear, and I want you to *know* that our Lord Jesus Christ longs to plant the kiss of forgiveness and healing upon your heart."

She said, "But no one has kissed me since I was a child, and Mother kissed me then." The dedicated Salvationist proceeded to share the gospel story with this unhappy woman. Eventually the woman surrendered her heart to God and became a Christian.

No Victory Without Struggle

Triumph without conflict is impossible. Some have mistakenly described Paul's lament over human weakness in Romans 7 as the experience of an unconverted Christian. This could not be, because Paul states in verse 22, "I delight in the law of God after the inward man." So the heart has been renewed. Paul is writing about himself and all born-again Christians. He is a converted follower of Jesus. There is an inward man who delights in the law of God. Romans 7 actually describes the experience of every converted Christian who delights in the law of God, but finds himself still tied to a sinful body that clamors for indulgence.

The sinful human nature is still there, up until translation time. Paul was distressed because in his new nature he was inclined toward the right. In his old nature he was inclined to sin. He declared,

> I don't understand myself at all, for I really want to do what is right, but I can't. I do what I don't want to—what I hate. I know perfectly well that what I am doing is wrong, and my bad conscience proves that I agree with these laws I am breaking. But I can't help myself, because I'm no longer doing it. It is sin inside me that is stronger than I am that makes me do these evil things.
>
> I know I am rotten through and through so far as my old sinful nature is concerned. No matter which way I turn I can't make myself do right. I want to but I can't. When I want to do good, I don't; and when I try not to do wrong, I do it anyway. Now if I am doing what I don't want to, it is plain where the trouble is: sin still has me in its evil grasp (Romans 7:15-20, TLB).

But the end is not yet. Paul loses some battles. He states, "I love to do God's will so far as my new nature is concerned; but there is something else deep within me, in my lower nature, that is at war with my mind" (verses 22, 23, TLB). In verses 24 and 25, Paul bursts out in near despair and cries, "Oh, what a terrible predicament I'm in! Who will free me from my slavery to this deadly lower nature? Thank God! It has been done by Jesus Christ our Lord. He has set me free." Another rendering is, "It will be done." What does Paul mean by that? "Those who follow after the Holy Spirit find themselves doing those things that please God" (Romans 8:5, TLB).

This is an escape experience. Second Peter 1:4 says, "Having escaped the corruption that is in the world through lust." Prisoners in state penitentiaries find themselves scheming to escape—to build tunnels under the wall, to climb fences, anything, just to get out and to be *free*!

For the prisoners of sin, Jesus has the key to unlock the gates and free us all. And that old jailer Satan can't stop Him. In the synagogue at Nazareth, Jesus declared, "The Spirit of the Lord is upon me . . . to preach deliverance to the captives, and . . . to set at liberty them that are bruised" (Luke 4:18, 19).

Great as is the shame and degradation through sin, even greater will be the honor and exaltation through redeeming love. To human beings striving for conformity to the divine image there is imparted an outlay of heaven's treasure, an excellency of power, that will place them higher than even the angels who have never fallen.

"Thus saith the Lord, the Redeemer of Israel, and His Holy One, to him whom man despiseth, to him whom the nation abhorreth, . . . Kings shall see and arise, princes also shall worship, because of the Lord that is faithful, and the Holy One of Israel, and He shall choose thee." Isa. 49:7.

"For every one that exalteth himself shall be abased; and he that humbleth himself shall be exalted" (*Christ's Object Lessons*, 163).

Peter accents Paul's declaration of faith in Christ for the victory, "Grace and peace be *multiplied* unto you through the knowledge of God, and of Jesus our Lord" (2 Peter 1:2, emphasis added). This calls for a little arithmetic. Contrast multiplication with addition, for example: 4 + 4 = 8—that's addition; but 4 x 4 = 16, twice as much—that's multiplication. 8 + 8 = 16, but 8 x 8 = 64, four times as much; 16 + 16 = 32, but 16 x 16 = 256, eight times as much. 32 + 32 = 64, but 32 x 32 = 1024. Follow this simple arithmetic to its logical end, and you will see the role of the divine Spirit in the salvation process. Salvation is God's work alone. But to be saved, we must with open hearts reach out and welcome the gift.

Peter contrasts multiplication with addition, the divine with the human part. Multiplication outdistances addition in a remarkably convincing manner. But addition has its place. Says Peter, "Beside this, giving all diligence, *add* to your faith virtue; and to virtue knowledge; and to knowledge temperance; and to temperance patience; and to patience godliness; and to godliness brotherly kindness; and to brotherly kindness charity" (verses 5-7). There you have the human element, the addition part: faith must have virtue added to it.

Wrote Ellen White, "You are not to think that you must wait until you have perfected one grace before cultivating another. No; they are to grow up together, fed continually from the fountain of charity; every day that you live, you can be perfecting the blessed attributes fully revealed in the character of Christ; and when you do this, you will bring light, love, peace, and joy into your homes" (Ellen G. White Comments, *SDA Bible Commentary*, 7:943).

No wonder that this author declared, "The first chapter of Second Peter is full of instruction, and strikes the keynote of victory. The truth is impressively enforced upon the mind by the way it is presented in this chapter. Let us more abundantly recommend the study of these words, and the practicing of these precepts" (ibid., 942).

Again and again in this chapter, Peter identifies victory with the knowledge of God and of Jesus our Lord (see verses 2, 8). Indeed, at the close of the second epistle, he admonishes us to "grow in grace, and in the knowledge of our Lord and Saviour Jesus Christ. To him be glory both now and for ever. Amen" (2 Peter 3:18).

> We must learn of Christ. We must know what He is to those He has ransomed. We must realize that through belief in Him it is our privilege to be partakers of the divine nature, and so escape the corruption that is in the world through lust. Then we are cleansed from all sin, all defects of character. We need not retain one sinful propensity. . . .
>
> As we partake of the divine nature, hereditary and

cultivated tendencies to wrong are cut away from the character, and we are made a living power for good. Ever learning of the divine Teacher, daily partaking of His nature, we cooperate with God in overcoming Satan's temptations. God works, and man works, that man may be one with Christ as Christ is one with God. Then we sit together with Christ in heavenly places. The mind rests with peace and assurance in Jesus (Ellen G. White Comments, *SDA Bible Commentary*, 7:943).

Have We Forgotten?

Peter was a zealous teacher. In 2 Peter 1:9, he says that we may have "forgotten" that we were purged from our old sins. In verses 10 and 12, he urges diligence to make the calling and election sure. He did not wish to be negligent in leading Christian believers to remember these things so that they might know and understand them and be established in the present truth. In verse 13, he declares that as long as he is alive, he will exert himself to remind us of the promises that God has made to ensure our salvation.

"The memory is a treasurer," said Nicholas Rowe, "to whom we must give funds, if we would draw the assistance we need."

The Spectacle of Transfiguration

Peter recalls how on the Mount of Transfiguration he beheld the spectacle of Jesus' glorious transfiguration. He declares that the sight and sound of the voice on the mountaintop was awe-inspiring. Then he states a truth that the whole confused world needs to remember, especially in these last days: "We have also a more sure word of prophecy; whereunto ye do well that ye take heed, as unto a light that shineth in a dark place, until the day dawn, and the day star arise in your hearts" (verse 19).

The Word of God is more sure than our visual and auditory senses. What are you going to do when and if the "ghost" of your deceased father or mother appears in the glory of a heavenly being before your very eyes? I had that experience just about one month after my father was killed in an elevator accident in San Diego, California. It was about three in the morning. Suddenly, there was a bright glow at the foot of the bed. There he was, his figure covered with a golden aura, his face unperturbed and peaceful. It seemed to me as if he were saying, "Son, do not weep for your daddy. It's better over here where I am than where you are." Then it was all over. I didn't seem to be frightened at all. Soon I was back asleep, but the memory of that "visitation" remains with me and will remain as long as I live.

I didn't know in those early days, before I had been instructed on the state of the dead, that it was not my father. Now I know that it was a skillful impersonation by a fallen angel committed to deception.

Sights and sounds can be bewildering and deceptive. I came to believe the Word of God instead of the visual appearance of my "father" in my bedroom that memorable night. Now I know it was an angel of hell on a deceitful mission to plant the seeds of error in a young man's mind.

The Divine Source of Prophecy

Peter winds up this exciting chapter with instruction concerning prophecy and the interpretation of Scripture.

In verse 20, Smith and Goodspeed tell us that scriptural prophecy cannot be "understood through one's own powers." Moffatt indicates that a person cannot "interpret it by himself." Williams: "By one's own mind."

The Holy Spirit, who inspired the prophecy, gives guidance to the sincere seeker for truth, illuminating the mind and calling from the text the true meaning. "No prophecy ever originated because some man willed it" (Amplified Bible, verse 21). Moffatt tells us that "it was when carried away by the holy Spirit that the holy men of God spoke."

In volume 7 of the *SDA Bible Commentary,* Ellen White says,

I take the Bible just as it is, as the Inspired Word. I believe its utterances in an entire Bible. . . .

The Bible is written by inspired men, but it is not God's mode of thought and expression. It is that of humanity. God, as a writer, is not represented. Men will often say such an expression is not like God. But God has not put

Himself in words, in logic, in rhetoric, on trial in the Bible. The writers of the Bible were God's penmen, not His pen. Look at the different writers.

It is not the words of the Bible that are inspired, but the men that were inspired. Inspiration acts not on the man's words or his expressions but on the man himself, who, under the influence of the Holy Ghost, is imbued with thoughts. But the words receive the impress of the individual mind. The divine mind is diffused. The divine mind and will is combined with the human mind and will; thus the utterances of the man are the Word of God (944-946).

How wonderful is this condescension of God in giving us the Holy Scriptures!

The Lord speaks to human beings in imperfect speech, in order that the degenerate senses, the dull, earthly perception, of earthly beings may comprehend His words. Thus is shown God's condescension. He meets fallen human beings where they are. The Bible, perfect as it is in its simplicity, does not answer to the great ideas of God; for infinite ideas cannot be perfectly embodied in finite vehicles of thought. Instead of the expressions of the Bible being exaggerated, as many people suppose, the strong expressions break down before the magnificence of the thought, though the penman selected the most expressive language through which to convey the truths of higher education. Sinful beings can only bear to look upon a shadow of the brightness of heaven's glory (ibid., 946).

So in this blessed Book is obtained the knowledge of God. The knowledge of God with its promises provides us assurance of a perfect and complete salvation made possible to us by the grace of God, experienced by us in the response of faith. Yes, all things have been provided for our total redemption. Not a single one of us need lose his or her soul. We may all be saved at last.

"If you can look into the seeds of time," said William Shakespeare, "and say which grain will grow and which will not speak thou to me." Fulfilled prophecy is the mark of prophetic inspiration.

Suppose that you are a farmer endowed with prophetic powers. You invite your farmer friends to your home one beautiful morning. Taking them out to the field, you carry a handful of corn kernels. The furrow is prepared. You drop the seeds in one by one. "This one will grow," you predict. "This one also will grow, but this one will not. This next seed will sprout, but it will be destroyed by worms. The fifth will grow," and so on and on until you come to the last kernel, and you state that it, too, will produce.

Your friends look at you and express surprise. "How do you know these things? You talk like a prophet or the son of a prophet."

Your reply is simple and direct: "When the time comes for corn to grow, you be here and check each of these seeds that I have planted in this furrow." When the time comes, every detail of the prognostication is fulfilled. The first kernel is growing, so is the second, but the third dies in the sod. The fourth was destroyed by worms and so on. The predictions were accurate and fulfilled to the very letter.

Now, what would you say about a person like that? What could you say? Remember the words of the quote, "If you can look into the seeds of time, and say which grain will grow and which will not . . ." How true this is of the divine forecasts in Scripture and also of the Spirit of Prophecy writings.

We have a more sure word of prophecy. More sure than our senses. We may give heed to it until the day dawn and the Daystar arise in our hearts. It is our safety and our safeguard against the multiplied errors of these last days.

Chapter 8:

John 17

THE LORD'S SUBLIME PRAYER

The prayer of John 17 is a heart-tingling revelation of the warm intimacy that existed between the Son of God and His Father in heaven.

The twenty-six divisions of the chapter reveal also Jesus' fervent desire that His disciples might experience the same connection with the Father that He knew so well. Listen to His petition: "That they all may be one; as thou, Father, art in me, and I in thee, that they also may be one in us: that the world may believe that thou hast sent me" (verse 21). Continuing, He implored the Father, "I in them, and thou in me, that they may be made perfect in one; and that the world may know that thou hast sent me, and hast loved them, as thou hast loved me" (verse 23).

Philip Schaff's Testimony

The person of Christ is to me the surest as well as the most sacred of all facts; as certain as my own personal existence; yea, even more so: for Christ lives in me, and He is the only valuable part of my existence. I am nothing without my Saviour; I am all with Him, and would not exchange Him for the whole world. To give up faith in Christ is to give up faith in humanity; to believe in Him is to believe in the redemption and final glorification of men; and this faith is the best inspiration of a holy and useful life for the good of our race and the glory of God (Philip Schaff, *The Person of Christ*, 8).

This is the theme of this remarkable prayer—oneness. It is the bond of peace in the packaging of divine contentment with the elements of love and fellowship all brought together and sealed. What would be the result of this oneness? "That they might have my joy fulfilled in themselves" (verse 13).

David knew about this oneness with God. "Thou wilt shew me the path of life," he said; "in thy presence is fulness of joy; at thy right hand there are pleasures for evermore" (Psalm 16:11).

But we are getting ahead of ourselves. First of all, we need to understand a few of the differences that exist between this prayer of John 17 and another very important prayer recorded in the New Testament—the prayer that Jesus taught His disciples to pray in His Sermon on the Mount (see Matthew 6:9-13). Jesus taught these sixty-six familiar words in response to their request for some modality in their praying. "Lord, teach us to pray," they humbly requested (see Luke 11:1). Five times in the prayer Jesus taught them to pray, the Lord God is directly addressed. But eight times the reference is to "us" or "our" need.

John 17: The Lord's Prayer

The Lord's Prayer is recorded by the beloved disciple John in the seventeenth chapter of his gospel. It was the last prayer of Christ uttered in the disciples' presence, immediately following the instruction He gave to them in John, chapters 14 to 16.

First, Jesus taught them what was absolutely necessary for them to know if they were to become successful in their apostalate, though now they needed the glow, the sparkle, and the brilliant presence of Jesus in their lives and in their witnessing. The Lord Jesus prayed that the glory of God might linger upon them, just as it rested upon Him. He opened His prayer by pleading, "Father, the hour is come; glorify thy Son, that thy Son also may glorify thee" (verse 1). The hour ahead offered to Jesus nothing but the agony of the cross, but there, when the sacrifice was made, the whole universe might see the true depth of the divine love and character. There the universe would witness the glory of God's self-denying and self-revealing love. The glory that Jesus experienced in His sacrifice was to be experienced in the final ministry of His followers. For example:

Peter, when he was crucified upside down; Paul and James, when they were beheaded; Bartholomew, when he was flayed alive; Stephen, when he was stoned to death. Glorious character and true martyrdom are evidence of this divine love.

As Jesus glorified the Father, so the disciples glorified Jesus. "The glory which thou gavest me," said Jesus, "I have given them; that they may be one, even as we are one: I in them, and thou in me, that they may be made perfect in one; and that the world may know that thou hast sent me, and hast loved them, as thou hast loved me" (verses 22, 23).

The Lord Jesus was the theme of the disciples' teaching and living. He was their song, their all in all. No wonder three thousand were baptized at Pentecost. The disciples related the story of the cross, the sacrifice, the resurrection. The Lord added to the church every day people who were being saved by His grace (see Acts 2:22-36; 3:12-26).

An Intercessory Masterpiece

Jesus' prayer was a mediatorial model, an intercessory masterpiece. It was a miniature of the work He must assume upon His ascension that He undertook for man as High Priest in the sanctuary above (see 1 Timothy 2:5; Hebrews 8:1-13).

This chapter [John 17] contains the intercessory prayer offered by Christ to His Father just before His trial and crucifixion. This prayer is a lesson regarding the intercession that the Saviour would carry on within the veil, when His great sacrifice in behalf of men, the offering of Himself, should have been completed. Our Mediator gave His disciples this illustration of His ministration in the heavenly sanctuary in behalf of all who will come to Him in meekness and humility, emptied of all selfishness, and believing in His power to save (Ellen G. White Comments, *SDA Bible Commentary*, 5:1145).

Jesus' prayer was an example of selflessness. The glory of the Father was the goal He sought. The success of the disciples was the centerpiece of His intercession. Christ wished to be glorified, not that honor would be given to Him on earth but that the Father might be glorified and honored.

Hannah's Prayer

There are many beautiful prayers recorded in the Bible. Take Hannah's prayer, for example, recorded in 1 Samuel 1. Her prayer was answered. It was a good prayer that concerned Hannah and her barrenness. It's good to take personal problems to the Lord. She badly wanted a child, a male child. In her bitterness of soul, she prayed to the Lord "and wept sore" (1 Samuel 1:10). She even vowed to the Lord that if He would look on the affliction of His handmaid, if He would remember her, if He would not forget her but would give her a man child, then she would give him to the Lord all the days of his life. He would become a Nazarite, and no razor would come upon his head. God answered her prayer. Samuel was born. He became the judge of Israel, one of the greatest of prophets.

Hannah's prayer is recorded in the Scripture to remind us that when we have bitterness of soul, when we have personal problems of vast dimensions, we can turn to the Lord, and He will answer our prayers. The Lord God has many names: *Elohim, Yahweh, El Shadi, Adonai, El Rorre, Jehovah Sabaoth*. This last name appears to be the name God's people appeal to when they suffer reverses, afflictions, weaknesses, failures, and defeats. In 1 Samuel 1:11, it is to *Jehovah Sabaoth* that Hannah appeals. Provoked by her adversary because she was barren, "in bitterness of soul" she "wept sore" and prayed, "O Lord of Hosts, if thou wilt indeed look on the affliction of thine handmaid, and remember me, and . . . will give unto thine handmaid a man child, then I will give him unto the Lord all the days of his life" (1 Samuel 1:11).

The Lord of Hosts, Jehovah Sabaoth—God indeed answers His children's prayers when they are offered in desperation. Take the prophet Jeremiah, for example; how urgently and sorrowfully and plaintively did Jeremiah appeal to the name of *Jehovah Sabaoth*, eighty-eight times in his book alone. The Lord of Hosts indeed answers the prayers of His children.

When David went out against Goliath, who defied the God of

Israel, he said, "Thou comest to me with a sword, and with a spear, and with a shield: but I come to thee *in the name of the Lord of hosts*, the God of the armies of Israel, whom thou hast defied" (1 Samuel 17:45, emphasis added).

Jesus' Great Concern

But Jesus faced giants of difficulty greater than Hannah's or David's. Before Him, in a matter of hours, was Mount Calvary—and the cross. He knew this, and in the first words of His model prayer, He prayed, "Father, the hour is come" (John 17:1). He had come to earth for this hour. But His concern now was not with Himself as much as His disciples. In Gethsemane He would pray for Himself.

Now His disciples are center stage. The triumph of His kingdom is uppermost in His mind. Selflessly He pleads to be glorified for one purpose, that the Father might be glorified through Him. He asks that this glory may rest upon the disciples, not for their sakes, but for the glory of God and the salvation of souls. "For their sakes I sanctify myself," He tells the Father, "that they also might be sanctified through the truth" (verse 19). He couldn't quit now. His hour had come, but the sacrifice had not yet been made. He declares His purpose to God—I'm not going to give up. It's too late in the day. I'm going through to total victory. Why? If I fail, the world will be lost. If I give in to the world, the flesh, and the devil, the plan of salvation will be frustrated, and the world will have no Saviour.

The disciples were with Jesus. They caught the spirit of His life, which interpreted His prayer. Just before Jesus uttered this prayer, they said, "Now are we sure that thou knowest all things, and needest not that any man should ask thee: by this we believe that thou camest forth from God" (John 16:30).

Power to Change in the Word

And how is sanctification to take place? Jesus prayed, "Sanctify them through thy truth: thy word is truth." "I have given them thy word" (John 17:17, 14).

It was the Word of God that sanctified the apostles. They were not of the world, even as Christ was not of the world.

Through the words of Christ, they were made clean (see John 15:3). Jesus' prayer for them was answered: "I pray not that thou shouldest take them out of the world, but thou shouldest keep them from the evil" (John 17:15).

What a sanctifying influence and power is found in the Word!

Dr. W. W. Watkinson recounts a Jewish legend relating to an act of the prophet Ezekiel. It seems that this great prophet raised several countrymen from the dead. It was, however, an imperfect miracle. The resuscitated men ever after retained the complexion of corpses, and their garments never lost the smell of the sepulcher. Dr. Watkinson declares that some people believe it is after this fashion that the Lord Jesus raises us from the death of sin to the life of righteousness. That, so far as our earthly lifetime is concerned, we must retain the blemishes and the scent of moral corruption. But, says this dynamic preacher, "we have not so learned Christ. We believe in his ability and purpose to cleanse us from every defilement, and to keep us in perfect purity of flesh and spirit."

Selflessness. That is the name of the prayer. Listen to these words of our divine Lord: "Father, I will that they also, whom thou hast given me, be with me where I am; that they may behold my glory, which thou hast given me: for thou loved me before the foundation of the world" (John 17:24). How eagerly and earnestly Jesus desired the disciples to behold with joy His great glory! Soon they were to face the agony of separation from their Leader, after witnessing His cruel death and the barbarous treatment received from His persecutors. Think of the utter desolation that they felt, as expressed by the two disciples on the way to Emmaus. "We trusted," they said to their Companion, "that it had been he which should have redeemed Israel: and beside all this, to day is the third day since these things were done" (Luke 24:21).

The structure of Christianity, so recently erected, had been burned to the ground in the fires of a great tragedy. All that remained were the ashes. The disciples were defeated, forlorn, hopeless; but, phoenixlike, Jesus sought to raise their hopes. He was thinking of them again. "O Father," He pleads, "let them see the glory I had with You before the world was. Let them see me as King of kings and Lord of lords, not as a crucified male-factor. Seat them on thrones next to Mine [see Matthew 19:27-30.] Let the painful scenes of earth depart, and flood their minds with the glory sights of the victory of the cross and the resurrection morning."

Yes, *selflessness* is the name of the prayer. In this prayer Jesus declares, "I have manifested thy name unto the men which thou gavest me out of the world" (verse 6). He tells how "while I was with them in the world, I kept them in thy name" (verse 12). And again in verse 26, "I have declared unto them thy name, and will declare it: that the love wherewith thou hast loved me may be in them, and I in them."

Yahweh is the name of the one true God, the ever-existing One, the "I AM." This I AM is described by John the Beloved, who caught the spirit of love in a fuller way than any of the other disciples (see 1 John 4:7-11).

Most of the English names of God used in Scripture are derived from the Hebrew. They are designed to be "vehicles of revelation." *Yahweh Jehovah* (Lord) is the I AM of Exodus 3:14, 15, the true God of Israel's worship. Elohim is the "more general name for God." *Adonai* means "lord" and in its secular usage refers to a "human superior." *Yahweh Sabaoth* is the commander of the hosts of God, "the vast power at Yahweh's disposal in the angel hosts" (see *Evangelical Dictionary of Theology*, edited by Walter A. Elwell).

Love is always selfless, self-effacing, and circumspect. First Corinthians 13 proves that. And, now, said Paul, abide three things: love, faith, and hope. The greatest of these is love. He declares that we should wholeheartedly pursue it (see 1 Corinthians 13:13–14:1, Montgomery).

Oneness. The glory of God is seen in the love that He gives, in the love that is received, and in the love that is passed on (see John 17:21-23).

A woman missionary was talking to a group of native women in China about Jesus—His unselfish life and loving ministry to the sin-sick, the lepers, the poor, and the blind. One woman, deeply impressed, nudged a friend seated next to her. "I always thought," she said, "that there ought to be a God like that!"

When the Father and the Son and the salvation of sinners is the one principle and interest in our lives, as we are the supreme objects of the Lord's regard and care, then it can be said that He is in us and we are in Him!

God was in Christ, reconciling the world to Himself. "To wit, that God was in Christ, reconciling the world unto himself, not imputing their trespasses unto them; and hath committed unto us the word of reconciliation" (2 Corinthians 5:19).

The reconciled person becomes an ambassador. "As though God did beseech you by us: we pray you in Christ's stead, be ye reconciled to God" (2 Corinthians 5:20).

Here is oneness of activity, oneness of affection, oneness of thought, oneness of belief, oneness of mission, oneness of effort, oneness of strength, oneness of power, oneness of love!

This could not be unless God and human beings were voluntarily united. Jesus volunteered to become our Saviour. This made the union possible. People volunteer to accept and serve Christ. This makes it reality.

Internal life. That life is the breath of the Spirit of God in us. Christ dwells in us by the Spirit, which He has given us. "Hereby we know that he abideth in us, by the Spirit which he hath given us" (1 John 3:24).

One day a pastor stopped at the home of a family and arrived just as they were having worship. The father had encouraged the children to repeat Bible verses. Each child faithfully repeated a text. One little girl repeated John 3:16, "For God so loved the world, that he gave his only begotten Son, that whosoever believeth in him should not perish, but have *internal life*."

The pastor did not correct the little girl because if Christians are ever going to have everlasting life, they must first of all have the internal life of the Spirit.

Unity. Unity is the bond of peace and the packaging of divine contentment. It is not, however, ecumenism, which is built on a mutual faith, and that alone. Unity must be built on the Bible platform. What does the Word of God teach? Jesus said, "I have given them thy word. . . . Sanctify them through thy truth: thy word is truth" (John 17:14-17). He declared, "I am the way, the truth, and the life" (John 14:6).

The apostle Paul, who brought the truth of God and the gospel to the Thessalonians and to the Galatians, had no doubts that the gospel he taught was the power of God unto salvation. This gospel alone could bring unity. He marveled that the Galatians were "so soon removed from him that called you into the grace of Christ unto another gospel: which is not another; but there be some that trouble you, and would pervert the gospel of Christ" (Galatians 1:6, 7).

Paul was certain that the gospel he preached was not of humans but of God. "For I neither received it of man, neither was I taught it, but by the revelation of Jesus Christ" (Galatians 1:12).

To the Thessalonians, Paul was equally a frank and a tender shepherd. "If any man obey not our word by this epistle, note that man, and have no company with him, that he may be ashamed. Yet count him not as an enemy, but admonish him as a brother" (2 Thessalonians 3:14, 15). In the same chapter, he declared, "The Lord direct your hearts into the love of God, and into the patient waiting for Christ. Now we command you, brethren, in the name of our Lord Jesus Christ, that ye withdraw yourselves from every brother that walketh disorderly, and not after the tradition which he received of us" (1 Thessalonians 3:5, 6).

"Unity with Christ establishes a bond of unity with one another. This unity is the most convincing proof to the world of the majesty and virtue of Christ, and of His power to take away sin" (Ellen G. White Comments, *SDA Bible Commentary*, 5:1148).

Things will be constantly arising to cause disunion, to draw away from the truth. This questioning, criticizing, denouncing, passing judgment on others, is not an evidence of the grace of Christ in the heart. It does not produce unity. Such work has been carried on in the past by persons claiming to have wonderful light, when they were deep in sin. Heresy, dishonesty, and falsehood were all blended in them.

The present is a time of great peril to the people of God. God is leading out a people, not an individual here and there. He has a church on the earth, that abide in the truth;

and when we see . . . men . . . crying out against the church, we are afraid of them. We know God has not sent them, yet they ran, and all who do not accept their erratic ideas are denounced as warring against the Spirit of the Lord. All such things are in Satan's line, but the work of God will go forward while there are now and ever will be those who work directly against the prayer of Christ. The work will advance, leaving them with their satanic inventions far behind (*Selected Messages*, 2:79).

Unity comes only by diligent searching of the Scriptures and is based on this foundation alone, not on sentimental ambitions to see the popular and the evangelical churches united under one banner of a common faith in Christ as Lord and Saviour. This is not enough. Christ is enough, to be sure; but Jesus said, I am the way, the truth, and the life. If we would be saved at last, we must follow Him and Him alone. This oneness of which Jesus spoke should not be understood to mean sameness or parroting or phony and blind following of the Lord. His Word, the Bible, must be the cement that holds us all together.

Unity plus diversity. "Our minds do not all run in the same channel, and we have not all been given the same work. God has given to every man his work according to his several ability. There are different kinds of work to be done, and workers of varied capabilities are needed. If our hearts are humble, if we have learned in the school of Christ to be meek and lowly, we may all press together in the narrow path marked out for us" (*SDA Bible Commentary*, 5:1148).

The one-talent man was cast into outer darkness, where there was weeping and gnashing of teeth. All of God's servants are dealt with according to their response to the Word of God. Some are touched deeply and are moved by the love of God to great efforts and self-discipline. Others receive the words of Christ as if the knowledge were common and deserving of no special response. Each ought to do the best that he or she can with the power God imparts. So all will be brought into harmony and united in answer to the Lord's sublime Prayer.

Chapter 9:

Isaiah 58

THE TRUE FAST, THE TRUE CHURCH, THE TRUE SABBATH

The TV speaker brimmed with charisma, and his message was attractive and magnetic. He talked about power to change lives. "We can do it," he said, "if we just decide to. We all have resources within ourselves. We just need to know how to release the power!"

The speaker had the key to unlock that powerful resource present in every human being! Of course, the viewer would have to buy twenty-five tapes, at a cost of $179.00. His words were so well chosen and spoken with such conviction that hundreds of people, perhaps thousands, enrolled in his course and mailed in a check to cover the cost!

As I thought about it, my own yearnings for power were stimulated. However, my Bible training had taught me to look to God and not to humans. The rules for self-discovery and self-actualization are presented in Scripture (see the Old Testament book of Proverbs and the New Testament books of Acts and James). The power to change human life is divine, the TV speaker's appeal to the contrary notwithstanding. Real personality change is change inside out. A radiant new person is the product of a radical heart change!

Remember Nicodemus? Eloquent rabbis of that time competed with Jesus and presented a philosophy of life that offered hope for change, but Nicodemus had heard them all. He had never, however, heard anyone like the Teacher from Galilee. In a private interview at night, he declared, "Rabbi, we know that thou art a teacher come from God: for no man can do these miracles that thou doest, except God be with him" (John 3:2).

What was the Galilean's reply? Jesus answered, "Verily, verily, I say unto thee, Except a man be born again he cannot see the kingdom of God" (verse 3).

The power to change human life and character is divine, not human. Philosophers and psychologists can teach us a lot about human relationships, the mind, and personality, but the key to a change of heart and life is in the hands of Jesus.

In Isaiah, chapter 58, we see portrayed by the gospel prophet a godly people who have experienced the power of change. They are saints of the last days, Sabbath keeping Christians, ambitious to imitate Christ, to labor as He labored, to minister to the suffering, and to save lost souls. This comes about, not by polishing up the ambitions of people who might enroll in the TV speaker's self-improvement program, but by beholding the ineffably beautiful character of our Lord and following His example in life and ministry.

The remarkable personality growth that can be achieved by studying and practicing the rules prescribed by "life and personality builders" is worthwhile, but provides no miraculous, life-changing experience or transformation in lifestyle and life goals. Here is where Isaiah 58, with its dynamic and powerful language, dramatizes the difference between external and internal values—form and substance, ritual and reality.

The Jews Knew the Rules

The Jews of Isaiah's time knew the rules. They diligently practiced these rules, one of which was fasting. But there came no change in their lives as a result of abstinence from food. The Pharisee, for example, who stood in the temple and prayed with himself, boasting about his dedication to ritual—his frequent fasts and his good stewardship (see Luke 18:11, 12). But Jesus said he was bankrupt, and He commended a heartbroken publican who beat his breast and cried out to God for mercy because he was a sinner (see verses 13, 14).

Programs and rules are skeletons without flesh and blood. Jesus' rule was the creative, divine principle of loving God with all your heart and loving your neighbor with love as great as your love for yourself. Here is a full-bodied, healthy-looking reality for ministry. The Lord describes the work of the remnant church in the last days. Isaiah 58 tells us that God's remnant people share, and they proclaim. It is a twofold responsibility—ministry and message, doing and saying. In verses 6, 7, 9, and 10, God marks out the message, as well as the ministry and the doing. Verses 8 to 11 share the blessed results; and in verses 12 to 14, we see the message.

So important is the sharing and the doing and the ministry that Isaiah makes clear that if we neglect it, we are not His people; not sheep, but goats, a different species.

"Every soul whom Christ has rescued is called to work in His name for the saving of the lost. This work had been neglected in Israel. Is it not neglected today by those who profess to be Christ's followers?" (*Christ's Object Lessons*, 191).

Verse 12 describes the Seventh-day Adventist people at work, sharing and also preaching: (1) building the old waste places; (2) raising up the foundations of many generations; (3) repairing the breach; (4) restoring paths to dwell in. What does this fourfold work imply?

The Fourfold Ministry

1. Like Nehemiah and Zerubbabel, Joshua and Ezra, who built the walls of Jerusalem and the temple itself, the church of the last days is composed of builders repairing the damage done by the propagation of error. The teachings of apostate Christianity have made a wasteland. Like Nehemiah and Ezra, Zerubbabel and Joshua, we must build upon the ruins of a Jerusalem wrecked by heresy and false teaching. This implies that we have "present truth" to proclaim. Does it sound like spiritual pride to say, "We have the truth, God's truth, and we know it!" No, it is rather conviction and information—Bible knowledge discovered in long days and nights searching the Scriptures for light! The pioneers of the church, in six Bible conferences in 1848, with humility and diligence prayed and studied until the truth shone out from the Word, bright and clear.

It also implies that we are zealous in the proclamation of this truth. Scripture predicts the worldwide dissemination of the third angel's message with latter-rain power. The loud cry will go like fire in the stubble. Truth shall arise and flourish in place of error. God's temple will be rebuilt in the last days, and, indeed, is now under construction.

2. The remnant church raises up the foundation of many generations. Jesus is that foundation. Christ is the center and circumference of the message: Jesus, preexistent, incarnate, sinless, a ransom, resurrected, ascended, interceding, and coming again. This is the Christology of the third angel's message. Christ is glorified and honored as Lord, Saviour, Priest, Judge, and coming King. We cannot say enough good things about Him. We love Him!

3. The Sabbath keeping, remnant people restore the Sabbath of the fourth commandment to its rightful position as the keystone of the arch—God's holy law of Ten Commandments. The breach is repaired, and spectators can see that the opening in the archway is mended and filled by the exaltation of the biblical Sabbath in place of the papal Sunday. The breach is repaired at last.

The repair is now in progress, and as the truth about the true Sabbath becomes well known, a worldwide controversy will rage, and on this Sabbath-Sunday issue will be fought the single greatest battle in all church history. The scene of the struggle will be worldwide!

4. The church acts as the restorer of paths to dwell in. Present truth, as contained in the three angels' messages, becomes a subject of international interest—the theme of every conversation, the testing point for the churches of the world, and the keynote of the Adventist proclamation.

Here are given the characteristics of those who shall be reformers, who will bear the banner of the third angel's message, those who avow themselves God's commandment-keeping people, and who honor God, and are earnestly engaged, in the sight of all the universe, in building up the old waste places. Who is it that calls them, The repairers of the breach, The restorers of paths to dwell in? [God] . . .

Their names are registered in heaven as reformers, restorers, as raising the foundations of many generations (Ellen G. White Comments, *SDA Bible Commentary*, 4:1151).

True and False Religion

But we are getting ahead of our story. Verses 1 to 11 present a dramatic contrast between true religion and its prostitution. James, in the New Testament, identified true religion: "Pure religion and undefiled before God and the Father is this, To visit the fatherless and widows in their affliction, and to keep himself unspotted from the world" (James 1:27). False religion is the opposite, and distasteful to God—a form that denies the power of God to change human lives! Said the prophet Isaiah:

Hear the word of the Lord, ye rulers of Sodom; give ear unto the law of our God, ye people of Gomorrah. To what purpose is the multitude of your sacrifices unto me? saith the Lord: I am full of the burnt offerings of rams, and the fat of fed beasts; and I delight not in the blood of bullocks, or of lambs, or of he goats. When ye come to appear before me, who hath required this at your hand, to tread my courts? Bring no more vain oblations; incense is an abomination unto me; the new moons and sabbaths, the calling of assemblies, I cannot away with; it is iniquity, even the solemn meeting. Your new moons and your appointed feasts my soul hateth: they are a trouble unto me; I am weary to bear them. And when ye spread forth your hands, I will hide mine eyes from you: yea, when ye make many prayers, I will not hear: your hands are full of blood (Isaiah 1:10-15).

Here a vital, life-giving change is called for. Not more rules and regulations, not more tapes, not more charismatic figures to captivate the imagination and tickle the emotions; no, but a change inside and out. Said Isaiah:

Wash you, make you clean; put away the evil of your doings from before mine eyes; cease to do evil; learn to do well; seek judgment, relieve the oppressed, judge the fatherless, plead for the widow. Come now, and let us reason together, saith the Lord: though your sins be as scarlet, they shall be as white as snow; though they be red like crimson, they shall be as wool. If ye be willing and obedient, ye shall eat the good of the land: but if ye refuse and rebel, ye shall be devoured with the sword: for the mouth of the Lord hath spoken it (Isaiah 1:16-20).

But it is hard for a religionist, steeped in ritual, form, and ceremony to understand that the forms of religion do not rightly represent the substance of it. And the Lord says, "What is the chaff to the wheat?" (Jeremiah 23:28). False teaching is likened to chaff, and those who receive it as truth are represented as chaff (see Isaiah 33:11-14; Psalm 1:4; Matthew 3:12).

Yet they seek me daily, and delight to know my ways, as a nation that did righteousness, and forsook not the ordinance of their God: they ask of me the ordinances of justice; they take delight in approaching to God. Wherefore have we fasted, say they, and thou seest not? wherefore have we afflicted our soul, and thou takest no knowledge? Behold, in the day of your fast ye find pleasure, and exact all your labours (Isaiah 58:2, 3).

In Christ's time, the woman at the well of Jacob identified true worship with a geographical place—Mount Gerazim. The Jews opted for Jerusalem. That was the true venue. But what did Jesus say? "The hour cometh, and now is, when the true worshippers shall worship the Father in spirit and in truth: for the Father seeketh such to worship him. God is a Spirit: and they that worship him must worship him in spirit and in truth" (John 4:23, 24).

The Pangs of Hunger for God!

Fasting—abstinence from food on given days—served as a link in the chain of Jewish formalism and worship. To suffer and deny self must certainly gain God's attention and favor, they believed. "See, Lord, I am willing to endure the pangs of hunger for You!" But it was self-righteousness, a sort of self-punishment—a gastronomic kind of masochism!

Isaiah gives inspired counsel to Israel to denounce the error of the worshipers and their misconceptions. "Is it such a fast that I have chosen? a day for a man to afflict his soul? is it to bow down his head as a bulrush, and to spread sackcloth and ashes under him? wilt thou call this a fast, and an acceptable day to the Lord?" (Isaiah 58:5).

Then the Lord describes the very essence of true worship, the true fast that He has chosen. "Is not this the fast that I have chosen? to loose the bands of wickedness, to undo the heavy burdens, and to let the oppressed go free, and that ye break every yoke? Is it not to deal thy bread to the hungry, and that thou bring the poor that are cast out to thy house? when thou seest the naked, that thou cover him; and that thou hide not thyself from thine own flesh?" (verses 6, 7; see also Job 31:13-22; Matthew 25:31-40).

Abstinence From Wickedness

But the "fast" of true worship is more than the plentitude of philanthropy. It is also abstinence from wickedness. Verse 6 needs to be repeated here. "Is not this the fast that I have chosen? to loose the bands of wickedness, to undo the heavy burdens, and to let the oppressed go free, and that ye break every yoke?"

And who is it that snaps the chains of wickedness? Isaiah has the answer. It is the Messiah.

The Spirit of the Lord God is upon me; because the Lord hath anointed me to preach good tidings unto the meek; he hath sent me to bind up the brokenhearted, to proclaim liberty to the captives, and the opening of the prison to them that are bound; . . . To appoint unto them that mourn in Zion, to give unto them beauty for ashes, the oil of joy for mourning, the garment of praise for the spirit of heaviness; that they might be called trees of righteousness, the planting of the Lord, that he might be glorified. And they shall build the old wastes, they shall raise up the former desolations, and they shall repair the waste cities, the desolations of many generations (Isaiah 61:1, 3, 4).

Medical Missionary Work

"In this scripture [Isaiah 58] the work we are to do is clearly defined as being medical missionary work. This work is to be done in all places. God has a vineyard; and He desires that this vineyard shall be worked unselfishly. No parts are to be neglected. The most neglected portion needs the most wide-awake missionaries to do the work which, through Isaiah, the Holy Spirit has portrayed" (*Testimonies for the Church*, 8:218).

No one with the scantiest knowledge of the humanitarian services provided by our institutions of mercy can deny that Isaiah 58 embraces their activities. In addition, Isaiah 58 includes the individual messenger of mercy who is devoted to the community, his neighbors, and even his enemies, who need the hand of love and caring extended to them.

But what is the model, the guiding principle for this work of benevolence conducted by Adventist institutions of mercy? Indeed, what is the model for all individual Christians?

At the walkway entrance to the grounds between the Loma Linda University Church and the School of Dentistry is a cluster of figures created by a famous sculptor. The theme is the good Samaritan. Beautifully fashioned in stone stand the good Samaritan, the priest, the Levite, and the victim of robbery and battery. They are all dramatically portrayed. Here is the model for all benevolent work carried on either by institutions or individual Christians.

We are commanded to love our neighbors as ourselves. This command is not that we shall simply love those who think and believe exactly as we think and believe. Christ illustrated the meaning of the commandment by the parable of the good Samaritan. . . . How tenderly the Lord regards all who are suffering and in want. They are to be helped, not to be oppressed (Ellen G. White, *Review and Herald*, 18 December 1894).

The angels . . . are prepared to co-operate with human agents in relieving oppression and suffering. They will co-operate with "those who break every yoke," who "bring the poor that are cast out to thy house;" who, "when they see the naked, that thou cover him; and that thou hide not thyself from thine own flesh" (ibid., 1 January 1895).

And how does the benevolent model of the good Samaritan apply to the rank and file?

God gives to every Christian a field or a work bench, but provides no easy chair. The excuse so often heard, "I have no time for Christian help work, no time to think of medical missionary work, no time to think of my neighbors; I have all I can do in looking after my own affairs," means, no time for God and humanity; it means all the time for self and the world. O, that we all might be able to join in the petition of one who prayed:

"O, Lord, that I may spend myself for others,
With no ends of my own;
That I may pour myself into my brothers,
And live for them alone."

Each of us has sometime greatly felt the need of a friend. How many of us are filled with an equally intense longing to some friendless one?

"Those who receive Christ as a personal saviour, choosing to be partakers of His suffering, to live His life of self-denial, to endure shame for His sake, will understand what it means to be a genuine medical missionary" (*Testimonies for the Church*, 8:209).

Then the promise is given to those in whose hearts God has produced a new life and this new ministry of compassion.

Then shall thy light break forth as the morning, and thine health shall spring forth speedily: and thy righteousness shall go before thee; the glory of the Lord shall be thy reward. Then shalt thou call, and the Lord shall answer;

thou shalt cry, and he shall say, Here I am. If thou take away from the midst of thee the yoke, the putting forth of the finger, and speaking vanity; and if thou draw out thy soul to the hungry, and satisfy the afflicted soul; then shall thy light rise in obscurity, and thy darkness be as the noon day: and the Lord shall guide thee continually, and satisfy thy soul in drought, and make fat thy bones: and thou shalt be like a watered garden, and like a spring of water, whose waters fail not (Isaiah 58:8-11).

It is in Jesus and in the performance of heart religion that rest is found (see Matthew 11:18-20). Indeed, the Sabbath of the fourth commandment becomes the sign or the seal of this latter-day remnant church, this caring, ministering church, this church that has found rest in Jesus.

If thou turn away thy foot from the sabbath, from doing thy pleasure on my holy day; and call the sabbath a delight, the holy of the Lord, honourable; and shalt honour him, not doing thine own ways, nor finding thine own pleasure, nor speaking thine own words: then shalt thou delight thyself in the Lord; and I will cause thee to ride upon the high places of the earth, and feed thee with the heritage of Jacob thy father: for the mouth of the Lord hath spoken it (Isaiah 58:13, 14).

"The soul who keeps the Sabbath is stamped with the sign of God's government, and he must not dishonor this sign. By closely examining the word of God, we may know whether we have the King's mark, whether we have been chosen and set apart to honor God" (*Medical Ministry*, 123).

Seventh-day Adventists are pinpointed in Isaiah 58 as: (1) Christians in life, in thought, in manner; (2) as Christlike in labor for the poor, homeless, and oppressed; (3) as "medical missionary workers"; that is, imitators of Jesus' methods of ministry to the whole person—body, soul, and spirit; (4) as faithful Sabbath keepers, whose example calls attention to Christ as Creator and Redeemer.

Chapter 10:

Matthew 24

WHEN SHALL THESE THINGS BE?

Think of the night sky, symbolically speaking, as a firmament of signs of the times announcing Jesus' soon return. It is filled with flashing lights and loud colors; with troublesome smog and haunting noises that leave us both startled and angry. Here is just one blasphemous and nauseating example, according to one review: American novelist Gore Vidal's book, *Live From Golgotha*, is a satirical novel about the crucifixion of Jesus Christ. According to Vidal, Jesus "tricked the Romans into crucifying Judas in his place," and the Jesus whom Paul saw on the road to Damascus was actually "Judas; an obese, ugly figure." Paul has a "homosexual affair with young Timothy." Jesus is "a thin, fire-breathing zealot who turns up in the twentieth century with bad teeth and a blueprint for Armageddon." The book is a moral affront to Christians in the same way that *The Satanic Verses*, by Salman Rushdie, offended Muslims. To top it off, Vidal comments that Christianity "is the greatest disaster ever to befall the West." Here is a literary source worse in Satanic influence than the false Christs and prophets about whom Jesus prophesied in Matthew 24, Mark 13, and Luke 21.

The great Teacher's prophecy of Matthew 24 encompasses the Christian age. The alpha of Jesus' prophecy embraced the omega of the Jewish nation as God's peculiar people, while the omega of the prophecy pinpointed the alpha of the new age, which would begin at the second coming of Christ. Yet generally speaking, the prophecy applies to the events that mark the end of the Jewish nation and the end of the world.

The historical context was decidedly gloomy. No welcome was ever extended to Jesus Christ, the Messiah, by the Jewish leaders, and the majority of the Jewish population spurned the Saviour. His presence was never celebrated by the race of people He came to redeem. They saw in Him "no beauty" that they should "desire him" (Isaiah 53:2).

And because He was not recognized as the One sent from heaven to redeem Israel, He became the "man of sorrows," the One who was "acquainted with grief" (verse 3).

If the foregoing was true of Israel at the time of Jesus' first advent, will the world of Christians, as they approach the time of His second advent, reveal the same characteristics? Tradition and ritual, the mere externals of worship, constituted religion for Israel in the time of Jesus. A form of godliness without the power thereof will also be characteristic of the churches in the last days (see 2 Timothy 3:1-5).

Bursting the Bubble of the Future

In Matthew 24, Jesus bursts the bubble of the future and reveals the events of centuries. Ellen White's multiplied comments on Matthew 24 fill a full page of references in the *Comprehensive Index* to her writings.

Jesus' forecast begins (verses 4, 5) with a warning against deceivers, who profess much but possess nothing. He concludes His masterpiece of divine prescience by describing the rebels against the truth of heaven, who will smite their fellow servants and find their pleasure with drunkards (verses 45-51).

In Matthew 24:15-20, Jesus describes the judgment upon Jerusalem, the city of the great King, whom the Jews had rejected. In the previous verses (5-14) of this monumental chapter, He designates the signs of the times that would precede the destruction of Jerusalem in A.D. 70. These events were to transpire within a period of four decades. They were also applicable to the period prior to the second coming of Christ.

Verses 6 to 10 outline the ugliest of all human experiences—wars (scores of them, big and little) and rumors of wars; the most widespread of human events—world war—nation against nation, kingdom against kingdom; the scariest of all disasters—

earthquakes; the most pitiful of tragedies—famines; the most feared of all catastrophes—pestilence; with tornadoes and tidal waves adding to the woe.

Earthquakes and Myriad Signs

Signs in the earth itself are multiplying thick and fast. In the last few months, since this manuscript was written, we have experienced two major earthquakes in Southern California; a tidal wave in Nicaragua; Hurricane Andrew in the Bahamas, Florida, and Louisiana—the worst tragedy ever to hit the United States; a typhoon in Guam; famine in Somalia, where two thousand starve to death daily; and civil war in the former Yugoslavia. The suffering human race longs for freedom from tragedy. The second coming of Christ is the answer to a dream of hope.

But specifically in verses 21 to 29, Jesus unfolds events to take place in succeeding centuries and immediately before His return. The strong, overmastering delusion will emerge in the carefully disguised appearance of false christs and false prophets, who will show great signs and wonders (verse 24). Finally, Satan himself appears as Christ. The deception will be so successful that even the very elect will have trouble making the distinction.

As the new age of Christ's glorious kingdom approaches, Satan will call to the front his own "New Age" prophets and advocates of a new and cosmopolitan religion, a rebaptized spiritualism. Jesus said it would happen. According to one report, 47,000 yuppies—young men and women successful in business—have adopted this deceptive new belief and been overwhelmed by it (see 2 Peter 3:2-7).

Randall N. Baer, a former top New Age leader, was rescued by a miracle of God's grace from this deceptive new teaching. In his book *Inside the New Age Nightmare*, he describes the New Age fruitage as appearing so glowingly golden, so delightfully compelling,

> so promising of peace, healing, and higher truths—yet underneath all the layers of gilded power and distorted truth is a rotten core of satanic bondage. People may enjoy a

host of apparent benefits—amazing out-of-body experiences, sometimes accurate psychic readings, apparently effective healings, temporary relief from some problems, etc.—but eventually the rotten core creeps more and more into the person's life. It is then that the demonic tentacles tighten their grip, the new ager's addiction to occult activities intensifies, and a harvest of dark fruit starts to corrode a person's life from the inside out.

Satan's Impersonation of Christ

But the overwhelming delusion of the end time will be Satan's impersonation of Christ.

The church has long professed to look to the Saviour's advent as the consummation of her hopes. Now the great deceiver will make it appear that Christ has come. In different parts of the earth, Satan will manifest himself among men as a majestic being of dazzling brightness, resembling the description of the Son of God given by John in the Revelation. Revelation 1:13-15. The glory that surrounds him is unsurpassed by anything that mortal eyes have yet beheld. The shout of triumph rings out upon the air: "Christ has come! Christ has come!" The people prostrate themselves in adoration before him, while he lifts up his hands and pronounces a blessing upon them, as Christ blessed His disciples when He was upon the earth. His voice is soft and subdued, yet full of melody. In gentle, compassionate tones he presents some of the same gracious, heavenly truths which the Saviour uttered; he heals the diseases of the people, and then, in his assumed character of Christ, he claims to have changed the Sabbath to Sunday, and commands all to hallow the day which he has blessed. He declares that those who persist in keeping holy the seventh day are blaspheming his name by refusing to listen to his angels sent to them with light and truth. This is the strong, almost overmastering delusion (*The Great Controversy*, 624).

Luke's Insightful Record

Luke records words that Jesus spoke that are not recorded by Matthew. (1) "Fearful sights and great signs shall there be from heaven" (Luke 21:11). (2) "Upon the earth distress of nations, with perplexity; the sea and the waves roaring; men's hearts failing them for fear, and for looking after those things which are coming on the earth: for the powers of heaven shall be shaken" (verses 25, 26).

It is Luke, also, who shares this warning with us:

(3) "Take heed to yourselves, lest at any time your hearts be overcharged with surfeiting, and drunkenness, and cares of this life, and so that day come upon you unawares" (verse 34).

Jesus indicated, "When ye shall see all these things, know that it [He] is near, even at the doors. Verily I say unto you, This generation shall not pass, till all these things be fulfilled. Heaven and earth shall pass away, but my words shall not pass away" (Matthew 24:33-35).

Will we heed these signs? Taking note of them is not enough. Being admonished by them and preparing for the second advent come closer to the target. And what was it that Jesus said? There will be "fearful sights and great signs . . . from heaven" (Luke 21:11).

Fulfilled prior to the destruction of Jerusalem in A.D. 70, these signs have meaning for us today. Note what happened in old Jerusalem:

Signs and wonders appeared, foreboding disaster and doom. In the midst of the night an unnatural light shone over the temple and the altar. Upon the clouds at sunset were pictured chariots and men of war gathering for battle. The priests ministering by night in the sanctuary were terrified by mysterious sounds; the earth trembled, and a multitude of voices were heard crying: "Let us depart hence." The great eastern gate, which was so heavy that it could hardly be shut by a score of men, and which was secured by immense bars of iron fastened deep in the pavement of solid stone, opened at midnight, without visible agency. . . .

For seven years a man continued to go up and down the streets of Jerusalem, declaring the woes that were to come upon the city. By day and by night he chanted the wild dirge: "A voice from the east! a voice from the west! a voice from the four winds! a voice against Jerusalem and against the temple! a voice against the bridegrooms and the brides! a voice against the whole people!". . . This strange being was imprisoned and scourged, but no complaint escaped his lips. To insult and abuse he answered only: "Woe, woe to Jerusalem!" "woe, woe to the inhabitants thereof!" His warning cry ceased not until he was slain in the siege he had foretold (*The Great Controversy*, 29, 30).

A Time of Distress and Despair

Commentary on these prophecies is almost superfluous. In our cities, people are scared to death, afraid to venture on the streets at night. In the city where I live, it is only October, and already four hundred persons have been murdered in drug wars and related crimes. Stress, fatigue, confusion of mind and doubt and uncertainty about the future take their toll on the human heart. Heart disease still kills more persons in the United States than any other disease. Los Angeles—in part—was a charred mess after the riots of 1992.

Jesus prophesied, "As the days of Noe were, so shall also the coming of the Son of man be. For as in the days that were before the flood they were eating and drinking, marrying and giving in marriage, until the day that Noe entered into the ark, and knew not until the flood came, and took them all away; so shall also the coming of the Son of man be" (Matthew 24:37-39).

"Christ declares that there will exist similar unbelief concerning His second coming. As the people of Noah's day 'knew not until the flood came, and took them all away; so,' in the words of our Saviour, 'shall also the coming of the Son of man be.' Matt. 24:39" (*The Faith I Live By*, 341).

Paul said, "Evil men and seducers shall wax worse and worse, deceiving, and being deceived" (2 Timothy 3:13). He also indicated in his second letter to Timothy that abominable crimes would be committed, not by evil-minded criminals alone but by church members:

> Understand this, that in the last days there will come times of stress. For men will be lovers of self, lovers of money, proud, arrogant, abusive, disobedient to their parents, ungrateful, unholy, inhuman, implacable, slanderers, profligates, fierce, haters of good, treacherous, reckless, swollen with conceit, lovers of pleasure rather than lovers of God, holding the form of religion but denying the power of it. Avoid such people (verses 5, RSV).

Pitiful, isn't it, that the jails and prisons—and homes of those murderers and other criminals who haven't been caught—should include people whose names appear on church records. Where is the power of God to keep Christians from crime? Lovers of pleasure more than lovers of God, they haven't found the joy of the Lord! If they had, they wouldn't resort to the world (see 1 John 2:15-17). In John's book of Revelation, the last-day apostate church is represented as a harlot—beautiful to behold and decked with jewelry (see Revelation 17:1-5). It is an accurate description.

A Judgment Is Required

The hour of God's wrath is near at hand, as well as the deliverance of the believing saints. A judgment is required in order to determine who, through faith in Christ and resulting obedience to His commandments, will be entitled to the gift of immortality and eternal life. An Adventist ventured from his pulpit to say that "if one is in Christ, there is no need of an investigative judgment." But who determines whether one is in or out of Christ if there is no investigative judgment? Jesus indicated that those who are found in Christ and overcomers will be taken and those who are found unfaithful will be left (see Matthew 25:40-42). All who have named the name of Christ will be judged (see 1 Peter 4:17, 18). This includes the priests and laypeople of Rome, as well as the ministers and laity of Protestantism. Seventh-day Adventists are included.

Daniel describes the activities of the little-horn power, the evil deeds, the persecutions, the change of the Sabbath, and the substitution of the Roman priesthood on earth for the ministry of Jesus, our High Priest, in heaven.

The Great Tribulation

The great tribulation that Jesus predicted is a matter of history:

> From Olivet the Saviour beheld the storms about to fall upon the apostolic church; and penetrating deeper into the future, His eye discerned the fierce, wasting tempests that were to beat upon His followers in the coming ages of darkness and persecution. In a few brief utterances of awful significance He foretold the portion which the rulers of this world would mete out to the church of God. Matthew 24:9, 21, 22. The followers of Christ must tread the same path of humiliation, reproach, and suffering which their Master trod. The enmity that burst forth against the world's Redeemer would be manifested against all who should believe on His name (*The Great Controversy*, 39).

Both the early church and the church of the Dark Ages experienced the fulfillment of this prophecy, written on the pages of history in blood. Fox's *Book of Martyrs* tells the story in startling verbiage, while James Wylie's *History of the Waldenses* and *The Papacy* and Merle D'Aubigné's volumes reinforce the accuracy of the tragedies that occurred. The only offense of those who died at the stake, were impaled, crucified, or flayed alive was their faith in Christ and His inspired Word.

James Stalker once said,

> There is a great deal of persecution still going on in the world. In every city there are works and shops where anyone making a decided profession of Christianity has to run the gauntlet of ridicule and annoyance; and there are homes, too, in which under the safe cover of what ought to be tender relationships, the stabs of aversion and malignity are dealt in the dark (*Best Modern Illustrations*, 266).

Signs in the Heavens

Christ's words about the great tribulation in Matthew 24:22—"those days," which were to be shortened—were descriptive of the period of 1,260 days (years) mentioned in Revelation 12 as the time when the dragon (Satan) would afflict the woman, representing the church. These days were to be cut short, and they were (see Mark 13:24, 25). The total period beginning A.D. 538 and ending A.D. 1798 was cut short about the time of the American Revolution. Shortly after 1776, the signing of the Declaration of Independence, the prophecy about which Jesus spoke was fulfilled. "In those days, after that tribulation, the sun shall be darkened, and the moon shall not give her light, and the stars of heaven shall fall" (Mark 13:24, 25). The dark day of May 19, 1780, the moon turning that night to the color of blood, and the falling stars, on the night of November 12 to 13, 1833, are historical monuments to the accuracy of Jesus' words. The great earthquake of November 1, 1755, which centered in Lisbon, Portugal, shook the greater part of Europe and Africa, and fulfilled the prophecy of Revelation 6:12.

The Time Is Ripe

These signs were intended to arouse people from their stupor and lead them to prepare for the coming of the Lord. The time is ripe to cry out:

> Blow ye the trumpet in Zion, and sound an alarm in my holy mountain: let all the inhabitants of the land tremble: for the day of the Lord cometh, for it is nigh at hand. . . . Sanctify a fast, call a solemn assembly: gather the people, sanctify the congregation, assemble the elders, gather the children, . . . let the bridegroom go forth of his chamber, and the bride out of her closet. Let the priests, the ministers of the Lord, weep between the porch and the altar. . . . Turn ye even to me with all your heart, and with fasting, and with weeping, and with mourning: and rend your heart, and not your garments, and turn unto the Lord your God: for he is gracious and merciful, slow to anger, and of great kindness (Joel 2:1, 15-17, 12, 13).

All of the minor prophets join their own rebuke for the sins of the people together with promises of God's mercy and forgiveness. Nearly every book closes with the beautiful assurance of pardon and acceptance (e.g., Hosea 14; Joel 3:17-21).

Jesus' great prophecy closes with a parable and this solemn warning, "Know this, that if the goodman of the house had known in what watch the thief would come, he would have watched, and would not have suffered his house to be broken up. Therefore be ye also ready: for in such an hour as ye think not the Son of man cometh" (Matthew 24:43, 44).

Singleheartedness of purpose should characterize the Christian's race for eternal life. Every habit that leads to sin and brings dishonor upon Christ ought to be put away, whatever the sacrifice.

> The blessing of heaven cannot attend any man in violating the eternal principles of right. One sin cherished is sufficient to work degradation of character, and to mislead others. . . . Not one who complies with the conditions will be disappointed at the end of the race. Not one who is earnest and persevering will fail of success. The race is not to the swift, nor the battle to the strong. The weakest saint, as well as the strongest, may wear the crown of immortal glory. All may win who, through the power of divine grace, bring their lives into conformity to the will of Christ (*The Faith I Live By*, 369).

"We can have a clean record in heaven today, and know that God accepts us; and finally, if faithful, we shall be gathered into the kingdom of heaven" (Ellen G. White Comments, *SDA Bible Commentary*, 7:989).

Chapter 11:

Revelation 14

THREE LAST MESSAGES—REALITY, NOT FABLE!

The good news and the bad news—that is the substance of the twenty spectacular verses of Revelation 14, with their powerful imagery and symbols and their solemn warnings to earth's last-day people.

Six angels with powerful messages for planet Earth and its last-time population are portrayed flying through the heavens above. Angels of mercy (verses 6-12) are sent to beast worshipers who do not know that they are victims of deception, but who now are given opportunity to repent and turn to God and the truth of the everlasting gospel. Three other angels—messengers of final judgment (verses 14-20)—are sent: one to give the call to gather the saints to their eternal reward (verses 14-16) and the other two to proclaim eternal separation from God to the disobedient. It all has the ring of solemn alarm, and we must search out its meaning; but first, let's lay some important groundwork.

Earthquakes and Church Attendance

Years ago, on the Hawaiian island of Kauai, our mission bungalow began to reel as a shock wave rolled across the foundation. We stood in the open door and prayed. Then I said to my wife, "Honey, I'm going to check with the telephone operator and ask a few questions."

It was a party line, and someone had beaten me to the phone—two island boys. "Did you feel the earthquake?" one of them questioned in a trembling voice.

"Yes," the other replied with bated breath. "I'm scared. I'm going to church tomorrow." If it wasn't so serious, it would have been amusing. I thought, It takes an earthquake to get some people back to church.

In Isaiah's prayer (chapter 26), he prays to the God who made the earth, "In the way of thy judgments, O Lord, have we waited for thee. . . .

With my soul have I desired thee in the night; yea, with my spirit within me will I seek thee early: for when thy judgments are in the earth, the inhabitants of the world will learn righteousness" (Isaiah 26:8, 9). God's judgments can have a staggering effect, and we fall on our knees! When we consider what is yet in store for planet Earth (Revelation 16), we tremble and wonder how we can find a way of escape!

Yet there are comparatively few casualties in these present tragedies that strike our cities and towns. Why is this? Peter answers, "The Lord is not slack concerning his promise, as some men count slackness; but is longsuffering to us-ward, not willing that any should perish, but that all should come to repentance" (2 Peter 3:9). Earthquakes and tidal waves, tornadoes and hurricanes, cause some serious thinking.

God has a purpose in permitting these calamities to occur. They are one of His means of calling men and women to their senses. By unusual workings through nature God will express to doubting human agencies that which He clearly reveals in His Word. . . .

How frequently we hear of earthquakes and tornadoes, of destruction by fire and flood! . . . Apparently these calamities are capricious outbreaks of disorganized, unregulated forces of nature, wholly beyond the control of man, but in them all God's purpose may be read. They are among the agencies by which He seeks to arouse men and women to a sense of their danger (Ellen G. White, *Last Day Events*, 28).

The merciful, compassionate God warns the world of impending conflicts. In the realm of the earthquake expectation, people are fearful of "The Big One." According to seismologists, the Pacific plates that rub against each other beneath the great San Andreas and other faults will soon build up enough pressure to split the crust of the earth, pop up, and destroy towns and cities. But will people heed the warnings? Are earthquakes just natural disasters, phenomena to be explained away by science?

Said Isaiah, "Let favour be shewed to the wicked, yet will he not learn righteousness: in the land of uprightness will he deal unjustly, and will not behold the majesty of the Lord. Lord, when thy hand is lifted up, they will not see" (Isaiah 26:10, 11).

But we must not blame earthquakes, tidal waves, hurricanes, and tornadoes upon God, though a few drops from the vials of God's wrath have already fallen on the earth. When He permits the elements to move contrary to natural law, it is so people may be awakened to their peril and seek the Lord for protection and care and to encourage them to turn to the Scriptures to find the meaning of calamity.

"These things are the result of drops from the vials of God's wrath being sprinkled on the earth, and are but faint representations of what will be in the near future" (*Last Day Events*, 27).

Satan To Blame!

Satan is a great mover of the elements.

> Satan works through the elements. . . . to garner his harvest of unprepared souls. He has studied the secrets of the laboratories of nature, and he uses all his power to control the elements as far as God allows. . . . Even now he is at work. In accidents and calamities by sea and by land, in great conflagrations, in fierce tornadoes and terrific hailstorms, in tempests, floods, cyclones, tidal waves, and earthquakes, in every place and in a thousand forms, Satan is exercising his power. He sweeps away the ripening harvest, and famine and distress follow. He imparts to the air a deadly taint, and thousands perish by the pestilence. *These visitations are to become more and more frequent and disastrous. Destruction will be upon both man and*

> beast. . . . "*The earth also is defiled under the inhabitants
> thereof; because they have transgressed the laws, changed
> the ordinance, broken the everlasting covenant*" (*The Great
> Controversy*, 589, 590, emphasis added).

"The wickedness of the inhabitants of the world has almost filled up the measure of their iniquity. This earth has almost reached the place where God will permit the destroyer to work his will upon it" (*Last Day Events*, 41).

The Saviour's Forecast

In prophetic vision, Christ visualized the very times in which we live and the reaction of people to the tempest of life. "Upon the earth distress . . . with perplexity. . . . Men's hearts failing them for fear, and for looking after those things which are coming on the earth" (Luke 21:25, 26).

Jesus then gave the promise, "Then shall they see the Son of man coming in a cloud with power and great glory. And when these things begin to come to pass, then look up, and lift up your heads; for your redemption draweth nigh" (verses 27, 28).

Messages Geared to the Hour

And not only is "the fact of His return" stated clearly and emphatically in Scripture, the Bible shows that God will provide a basis for hope in a triple message geared to these final hours of time. Revelation 14 is the depository of the three angels' messages—earth's final warning system—now being sounded by God's commandment-keeping people with a resonance, a volume, a clarity, matching the solemn and sacred pronouncements of John the Baptist concerning the Messiah, Jesus Christ, at His first advent.

Think for a moment of John's spectacular performance. The Baptist was an *earthquake*! The people were shaken by his message. The fabric of self-righteousness cracked, broke, collapsed, and fell to the ground. The people were stunned into an awakening and a reception of Jesus as Lord and Saviour. Many accepted his message and became the first Christians.

Today it's urgent that the Seventh-day Adventist Church do

some self-shattering appraisal and some powerful witnessing. All of us should be earthquakes of a sort. John the Baptist registered an 8 or a 9 on the Richter scale. We may—some of us—do enough to make a 6 or a 7—maybe only a 5 or even a 3 or 4, but we ought to be doing something startling! What is heaven's seismograph saying about us? "Awake to righteousness, and sin not; for some have not the knowledge of God: I speak this to your shame" (1 Corinthians 15:34).

As John prepared the way for Christ at His first advent, God has raised up Seventh-day Adventists with the Elijah message of preparation for the return of Jesus, the glorious second advent. And with the close of probation near and the time of trouble within an uncomfortable distance, we ought to be waking up and making up for lost time.

A Latter-Day Fulfillment

Think of the three angels' messages as God's last call to this big bad world, while the Elijah message is God's last call to modern Israel. The first invites the "outsider" to become a part of God's family and join up with the household of faith; the second is God's urgent call for us to set our house in order and unite young and old in loyalty to God. The Laodicean message is God's diagnosis of our spiritual poverty and His cure for our condition (Revelation 3:14-22).

Different periods in the history of the church have each been marked by the development of some special truth, adapted to the necessities of God's people at that time. Every new truth has made its way against hatred and opposition; those who are blessed with its light were tempted and tried. The Lord gives a special truth for the people in an emergency. Who dare refuse to publish it? He commands His servants to present the last invitation of mercy to the world. They cannot remain silent, except at the peril of their souls (*The Great Controversy*, 609).

In these final days, the end time of the world, a time of universal iniquity and disregard of the moral law, God has a people who, like David, love God's law. Through the grace of Jesus Christ, they are enabled to be obedient to the two great precepts of love, which find expression in the ten precepts of God. "Here is the patience of the saints: here are they that keep the commandments of God, and the faith of Jesus" (Revelation 14:12). While some Christian leaders openly declare that commandment keeping is not possible, God points to an earthly group who, by His grace, keep His holy law.

Said Paul A. Cedar,

Not long ago, I was leading a small group of professional people in a Bible study on the Book of James. Within that context, I shared a word study on the word "faith" which is so central to the message of James. I contended that an appropriate Biblical definition for faith is "active obedience," and shared that God has called us to be His obedient servants. The initial response of those in the group was surprise and resistance.

Like many of us, they had fallen into the self-centered lifestyle. They did not wish to be servants of anyone nor were they excited about the lifestyle of obedience. Instead they preferred for God to fall into the flow of their lives and to subscribe to their wishes.

Of course, they were challenging one of the basic requirements of being a true Christian. To follow Jesus Christ as Lord in obedience and to serve Him is not an option for authentic Christian lifestyle; it is imperative (*The Communicator's Commentary: James, 1, 2 Peter, Jude*, 148).

God calls upon the earth and the inhabited universe to behold a people in defense of God's law, which they delight to obey. To them has been entrusted the three angels' messages described in Revelation 14:6-12. Believing and accepting fully the solemn warnings embraced in this triple message, they cannot help but share with others the unspeakably glorious truths contained in the three alarms. The power of the Latter Rain outpouring will bring the whole world to a knowledge of truth (see Joel 2:28-32).

The First-of-All Message

First of all, with hearts ablaze and tongues on fire, the angels proclaim the age-old message of the "everlasting gospel." They tell the old, old story of forgiveness without money or price through the redemption offered by Jesus Christ. These messengers of mercy, winged by love and truth and dispatched by the command of God Himself to fly in the midst of heaven, reach out to every nation, kindred, tongue, and people. It is a worldwide movement. What do they proclaim? "Fear God, and give glory to him; for the hour of his judgment is come: and worship him that made heaven, and earth, and the sea, and fountains of waters."

In the early mid-nineteenth century, preceding our own Seventh-day Adventist missionaries, preachers of God's appointment

appeared in different countries of Christendom at the same time. In both Europe and America, men of faith and prayer were led to the study of the prophecies, and, tracing down the inspired record, they saw convincing evidence that the end of all things was at hand. In different lands there were isolated bodies of Christians who, solely by the study of the Scriptures, arrived at the belief that the Saviour's advent was near (*The Great Controversy*, 357).

In 1818 William Miller, a New York farmer, arrived at his exposition of the prophecies pointing to the time of the judgment (initially, 1843). In 1821 Joseph Wolff, the "missionary to the world," began to proclaim the Lord's soon coming. Wolff was born in Germany of Jewish parents; his father was a rabbi. Studying the Scriptures, Wolff became a Christian and was especially attracted by predictions concerning the return of our Lord. His interpretation of the prophetic periods placed the great consummation within a very few years of the time pointed out by Miller.

In England, the great truth of Christ's return was extensively proclaimed. In South America, the message was given by Manuel de Lacunza, a Spaniard and a Jesuit. In Germany, the word was spread by Johann Bengel, a Lutheran minister. In France and Switzerland, Louis Gaussen preached the message.

The gospel was the theme of their preaching. "The hour of His judgment is come" was the setting in which the gospel proclamation was sounded, awakening the people to the truth that the return of Jesus was near and that His coming would be preceded by a heavenly examination of all the records. Worship God, the Creator of heaven and earth, was the solemn call.

Understanding these solemn truths didn't all happen in a day. As time went on, thoughtful people took out their Bibles to learn more about the Creator of heaven and earth. Their minds were directed back to the first two chapters of the book of Genesis and to the Sabbath, which commemorated the creation of the world in one week's time. It became clear to them that the observance of Sunday, the first day of the week, had created a breach in God's holy law and that humans' ordinances, substituting for God's, were not acceptable (see Isaiah 58:12-14).

"Babylon Is Fallen"

Those who continued to study God's Word came into possession of these great truths, while those who rejected the light were solemnly warned by the second angel's message that they had fallen from God's favor. "Babylon is fallen, is fallen, that great city" (Revelation 14:8).

When the Lord Jesus Christ did not appear as expected in 1844, these godly people wept bitterly. Why? Because they loved their Lord dearly and expected to be with Him in that better world. They truly loved His appearing. Rising from their disappointment, they went on to seek the reason, and they found it in the Scriptures (see Revelation 10).

Contrast this experience with that of thousands of Europeans in the last days of the year A.D. 999. The advent expectation was high. It was believed that before midnight on December 31 of that year, the end of the world would come, as would the judgment of all people and the advent of Jesus Christ in the clouds of heaven. It was the close of the first Christian millennium. Large numbers of people came to believe that all earthly things would soon terminate. The churches were crowded, and the people were delirious with fear. When midnight struck and nothing happened, there was hilarious rejoicing. No one really wanted to see Jesus come, and when the time passed, those who had offered the loudest prayers and exhibited the most emotional cries for mercy returned gleefully to their earthly pleasures and casual existence.

Today, we are standing deep into the decade that will witness the close of the second Christian millennium, the year 1999. Will history repeat itself? Will false teachers arise, setting dates and predicting the time for the end of the world? Already, we are beginning to witness evidence of this. Watch the headlines, and shy away from the prognosticators to avoid any more disappointments.

Who can guarantee that Christ's second coming will be delayed until the year 2000? Jesus told us to watch and pray, for we know not the hour. We know not when the time is, but God has mercifully made provision for a worldwide message to go with pentecostal power to the ends of the earth.

Now the time is ripe for the great outpouring of the Holy Spirit upon the earth to accompany the proclamation of the third angel's message. The message goes forth, "If any man worship the beast and his image, and receive his mark in his forehead, or in his hand, the same shall drink of the wine of the wrath of God" (Revelation 14:9,10).

There is a time sequence in the triple proclamation, as well as a continuum of proclamation. The messages, all three of them, will be present truth until the close of time.

The Beast Power Identified

"The solemn messages that have been given in their order in the Revelation are to occupy the first place in the minds of God's people" (*Last Day Events*, 16).

"I then saw the third angel [Rev. 14:9-11]. Said my accompanying angel, 'Fearful is his work. Awful is his mission. He is the angel that is to select the wheat from the tares and seal, or bind, the wheat for the heavenly garner. These things should engross the whole mind, the whole attention'" (ibid., 14).

It is not difficult to discover in church history the unusual religious and civil power that answers to the formidable beast power of Revelation 14. Daniel the prophet predicted that this agency of apostasy would think to change times and laws (see Daniel 7:25). It would substitute man-made ordinances for the commandments of God. The Roman Church fulfills the symbol completely. The hierarchy is pointed out—not the innocent members, many of whom would be horrified if they knew the history of the Roman establishment.

Who was it who took the second commandment out of the law that condemned image worship and thus made provision, without blame, for the continuation of the worship of images and the veneration of saints and angels? Who was it who substituted the observance of the first day of the week for the observance of the Bible Sabbath, the seventh day of the week? Answer: The Roman papacy. The warning is against this institution of rebellion against God's holy Word and the Ten Commandment law. So the wrath of God in the form of seven deadly plagues (Revelation 16) will be poured out upon those who persist in such worship. And how many are involved? Listen! "All the world marveled at this miracle and followed the Creature in awe" (Revelation 13:3, TLB). Someone has remarked that "all the great injustices of history have been committed in the name of unchecked and unbridled 'majority rule.' "

The late Senator James A. Reed, of Missouri, in one of the most forceful speeches ever delivered before the Senate, observed with great truth: "The majority crucified Jesus Christ; the majority burned the Christians at the stake; the majority established slavery; the majority jeered when Columbus said the world was round; the majority threw him into a dungeon for having discovered a new world; the majority cut off the ears of John Pym because he dared advocate the liberty of the press (*7000 Illustrations*, 328).

But there will be a minority who will emerge as God's remnant people (see Revelation 12:17).

But who is the "image of the beast," and what is the "mark"?

First of all, observe the lamblike, two-horned beast of Revelation 13:11, who, chameleonlike, turns color and speaks like a dragon—from the pure white raiment of the lamb, he "turns coat" and becomes the fiery red of the persecutor. This word-creature of prediction creates an image to the first beast; that is, it becomes like Rome; a persecuting power, a combination of church and state, but it is not Rome, it is apostate Protestantism in America.

One to whom God opened up the meaning of these prophetic symbols wrote at length on the question:

> When the Protestant churches shall unite with the secular power to sustain a false religion, for opposing which their ancestors endured the fiercest persecution; when the state shall use its power to enforce the decrees and sustain the institutions of the church—then will Protestant America have formed an image to the papacy, and there will be a national apostasy which will end only in national ruin (Ellen G. White Comments, *SDA Bible Commentary*, 7:976).

Notice that the Sabbath question will be central in the matter of the imposition of the seal of God or the mark of the beast:

> The Sabbath question is to be the issue in the great final conflict, in which all the world will act a part. Men have honored Satan's principles above the principles that rule in the heavens. They have accepted the spurious Sabbath, which Satan has exalted as the sign of his authority. But God has set His seal upon His royal requirement. Each Sabbath institution, both true and false, bears the name of its author, an ineffaceable mark that shows the authority of each.
>
> The great decision now to be made by every one is, whether he will receive the mark of the beast and his image, or the seal of the living and true God (ibid., 977).

The minor prophet Joel predicted that multitudes would be

in the valley of decision (see Joel 3:14). In these very days in which we live, thousands will accept the truth of the three angels' messages and link their lives and destiny with the Saviour, Jesus Christ, and with the people who keep His commandments. Others will reject the three messages and stubbornly persist in their old ways. A. Bannington has said that whenever you face a decision, you have three choices: "Do what you please, do what others do, or do what is right."

The right thing to do is to accept the messages.

"The third angel's message has been sent forth to the world, warning men against receiving the mark of the beast or of his image in their foreheads or in their hands. To receive this mark means to come to the same decision as the beast has done, and to advocate the same ideas, in direct opposition to the Word of God" (*SDA Bible Commentary*, 7:979).

"The people of the world are worshiping false gods. They are to be turned from their false worship, not by hearing denunciation of their idols, but by beholding something better. God's goodness is to be made known. 'Ye are My witnesses, saith the Lord, that I am God.' Isa. 43:12" (*Christ's Object Lessons*, 299).

Heaven is waiting for those who are faithful, who keep the commandments of God and the faith of Jesus. Those who face the specifications outlined in the three angels' messages and refuse to repent of their transgressions will realize the result of disobedience. So there is good news (see Revelation 14:6-12), and there is bad news (see verses 18-20). In this case, it is utterly unnecessary to be a part of the sad and bad news. All need not be lost! We may all be saved!

God extends to faithful Adventists the call:

Let no one yield to temptation and become less fervent in his attachment to God's law because of the contempt placed upon it; for that is the very thing that should make us pray with all our heart and soul and voice, "It is time for thee, Lord, to work: for they have made void thy law." Therefore, because of the universal contempt, I will not turn traitor when God will be most glorified and most honored by my loyalty (*SDA Bible Commentary*, 7:981).

Chapter 12:

Psalm 91

SAFE IN THE SECRET PLACE!

"He that dwelleth in the secret place of the most High shall abide under the shadow of the Almighty. I will say of the Lord, He is my refuge and my fortress: my God; in him will I trust" (Psalm 91:1, 2).

Luther was once asked if he had the faith of a martyr. "No," he replied, "but if God calls me to die for my Lord, He will give me the faith of a martyr."

Faith in God in times of trouble is the hallmark of the living as well as the dying saints.

This brings us to the ninety-first Psalm, which, like Psalm 46, was composed especially for end-time Christians.

Most theologians agree that Moses—a man who had seen much trouble—composed the lyrics of the ninetieth psalm. (Wouldn't it have been wonderful to have heard him sing the psalm!) Many think David wrote the ninety-first, but whether the ninety-first was authored by David or by Moses or someone else, one thing is certain; the ongoing theme of this powerful psalm is the protection afforded the saints of God in the final, dangerous days of human history.

It is a time of many snares and plagues, terrors, arrows of destruction, lions and adders, dragons and noisome pestilences.

Yes, but his song was not about the perils. It was concerned with protection from them. Glance down the psalm again, and note the words employed to describe that protection. "Refuge, fortress, pinions, wings, shield, buckler, angels, deliverance, honour, long life, satisfaction, salvation." Thus we find words that mark the perils, and words that tell of perfect protection from all those perils. That is the glory of psalm ninety-one (G. Campbell Morgan, *Great Chapters of the Bible*, 6, 7).

The Bible is accented with dramatic pictures of divine protection for the children of God—Daniel saved by the angels from the hungry, snarling lions (Daniel 6:10-23); Shadrach, Meshach, and Abednego safe in the fiery furnace, sheltered by the Son of God (Daniel 3:19-25); David, protected from the giant Philistine, Ishbibenob, by a gallant soldier on the battlefield (2 Samuel 21:15-21); Peter safely guided from the prison houses, the shackles falling miraculously from his wrists, while the guard slept (Acts 5:17-29). Can you not call up a time in your life when you were miraculously saved from death or injury! God is with us, and that's good news!

Wrote Ellen White:

In the ninety-first psalm is a most wonderful description of the coming of the Lord to bring the wickedness of the wicked to an end, and to give to those who have chosen Him as their Redeemer the assurance of His love and protecting care. . . .

In the time when God's judgments are falling without mercy, oh, how enviable to the wicked will be the position of those who abide "in the secret place of the Most High"—the pavilion in which the Lord hides all who have loved Him and have obeyed His commandments! The lot of the righteous is indeed an enviable one at such a time to those who are suffering because of their sins. But the door of mercy is closed to the wicked, no more prayers are offered in their behalf, after probation ends.

But this time has not yet come. Mercy's sweet voice is still to be heard. The Lord is now calling sinners to come to Him (*SDA Bible Commentary*, 3:1150).

Psalm 91 is for today as well as for the time of trouble.

Here is an exciting illustration:

A few years ago, in company with Dr. Alstrup Johnson, a long-time friend, I checked in for Pan Am Flight 843, San Francisco to Honolulu. The Boeing 707 four-engine jet held a full complement of passengers and a crew of ten. It was a bright July day, and with a feeling of confidence we bade my wife and daughter goodbye and went aboard. There was nothing to indicate trouble ahead. The takeoff was routine, and within minutes the giant plane was rocketing westward toward the vast Pacific Ocean. At that instant, Flight 843 became a nightmare. I felt a shock, then a shudder, and looking out from my window seat over the wing, I saw the right outboard engine aflame. The plane inclined sharply to the left, yawed wildly to the right, and the fire-alarm bell sounded. Terror-stricken passengers screamed. As we watched, the fiery engine burned loose and hurtled to the earth, leaving the stricken wing curling upward in ghastly trailing flames. Seconds later almost half the weakened wing fell off. Aerodynamically, Flight 843 should have crashed.

My companion and I clasped hands and prayed earnestly that God's will would be done. A half hour later, with piloting later praised as "masterful," Captain Kimes set the crippled plane down smoothly at Travis Air Force Base. Asked about it, he replied with feeling, "I had help from above." I agree with Captain Kimes.

We felt from this harrowing episode that God had "set His love" (Ps. 91:47) upon us. May this lesson come to all who read of our experience (Floyd O. Rittenhouse, *Show Me Thy Ways*, 228).

God's caring and sheltering is not appreciated as it might be:

The Lord works continually to benefit mankind. He is ever imparting His bounties. He raises up the sick from beds of languishing, He delivers men from peril which they do not see, He commissions heavenly angels to save them from calamity, to guard them from "the pestilence that walketh in darkness" and the "destruction that wasteth at noonday" (Ps. 91:6); but their hearts are unimpressed. He has given all the riches of heaven to redeem them, and yet they are unmindful of His great love. By their ingratitude they close their hearts against the grace of God. Like the heath in the desert they know not when good cometh, and their souls inhabit the parched places of the wilderness (*The Desire of Ages*, 348).

The Psalmist's Faith in God's Care

The first thirteen verses of Psalm 91 represent the psalmist's joyful and exciting testimony of God's care for those who dwell in the secret place. In response, God Himself endorses David's proclamation of trust by saying, "Because he hath set his love upon me, therefore will I deliver him: I will set him on high, because he hath known my name. He shall call upon me, and I will answer him: I will be with him in trouble; I will deliver him, and honour him. With long life will I satisfy him, and shew him my salvation" (verses 14-16).

The Governor of the universe here presents a medal of honor, a presidential medal, if you will; His own personal approval and reassurance that what David has said is absolutely true. It is impossible for God to lie, and as Paul tells us in Hebrews,

Wherein God, willing more abundantly to shew unto the heirs of promise the immutability of his counsel, confirmed it by an oath: that by two immutable things, in which it was impossible for God to lie, we might have a strong consolation, who have fled for refuge to lay hold upon the hope set before us: which hope we have as an anchor of the soul, both sure and stedfast, and which entereth into that within the veil; whither the forerunner is for us entered, even Jesus (Hebrews 6:17-20).

Let's look at God's promise and affirmation of approval in Psalm 91: (1) I will deliver him (verse 14); (2) I will set him on high (verse 14); (3) I will answer him (verse 15); (4) I will be with him in trouble (verse 15); (5) I will deliver him (verse 15); (6) I will honor him (verse 15); (7) With long life will I satisfy him (verse 16); (8) I will show him My salvation (verse 16). This delightful "octave" in the psalm is resonant with God's love and care for His people.

The Perils of David's Existence

In the eleventh psalm David writes, "For, lo, the wicked bend their bow, they make ready their arrow upon the string, that they may privily shoot at the upright in heart" (verse 2).

Here, David is describing the perils of his own existence, pursued by the jealous King Saul, his life in constant danger. David was at times overcome by sorrow and discouragement. He fled from Saul and found shelter under the protection of a Philistine lord, Achish (see 1 Samuel 21:10). On another occasion, in order to escape detection and apprehension by Saul, he lied to the priest of God, Ahimelech, and as a consequence occasioned the death of this holy man and his family (1 Samuel 21, 22).

David was far from perfect, but his life was not to be measured by the occasional good deed or misdeed but by the habitual tendency of his thoughts and his faith in God. He never ceased to trust in the Lord God of Israel, and in the eleventh psalm, he said in verse 1, "In the Lord put I my trust." David found his shelter in God, because he dwelt in the secret place of the Most High. He found himself safe abiding under the shadow of the Almighty.

In Hebrew language the word (abide) was used as expressing the idea of passing the night. "He that dwelleth in the secret place of the Most High, shall pass the night under the brooding wings of the Almighty." That is the whole idea of the psalm. . . . This psalm is not a psalm about still waters, but about storm and stress and strain. We know something about still waters. "He leadeth me beside still waters." But He does not always lead us there. Sometimes the waters are not still, they are storm-lashed. This psalm is the psalm of the storm; it is the psalm of the night. If we dwell in the secret place, we pass the night under the outspread pinions of God (G. Campbell Morgan, *Great Chapters of the Bible*, 74).

The Time of Jacob's Trouble

Like David in his flight from the anger of Saul and his army, God's remnant commandment-keeping people will find shelter in God. It is during the fearful time of Jacob's trouble that their lives are in the greatest danger. Probation has closed (see Revelation 22:11, 12); all about them, earth's final plagues are falling upon the wicked (see Revelation 16).

> A thousand shall fall at thy side, and ten thousand at thy right hand; but it shall not come nigh thee. . . . There shall no evil befall thee, neither shall any plague come nigh thy dwelling. For he shall give his angels charge over thee, to keep thee in all thy ways. They shall bear thee up in their hands, lest thou dash thy foot against a stone (Psalm 91:7, 10-12).

The final act of earthly governments will be the death decree, enacted to wipe out the church of God, the defenders of God's truth. Wrote Ellen White:

> Though a general decree has fixed the time when commandment keepers may be put to death, their enemies will in some cases anticipate the decree, and before the time specified, will endeavor to take their lives. But none can pass the mighty guardians stationed about every faithful soul. Some are assailed in their flight from the cities and villages; but the swords raised against them break and fall powerless as a straw. Others are defended by angels in the form of men of war.
>
> In all ages, God has wrought through holy angels for the succor and deliverance of His people (*The Great Controversy*, 631).

In the forty-sixth psalm, the psalmist speaks of this time when the mountains shall be moved and carried into the midst of the sea; when the waters roar and are troubled; when the heathen will rage, and God, as Chief Executive of the universe, interposes to make wars to cease unto the end of the earth. He breaks the bow and cuts the spear in sunder; He burns the chariot in the fire (verses 2, 3, 6, 9).

In Revelation 19, the Lord of Hosts is pictured as "The Word of God" coming forth seated upon a white stallion, with the angels of heaven following, likewise mounted and appearing as warriors. A sword proceeds out of the mouth of Jesus Christ, and the wicked are slain.

The words of the psalmist are fascinating. "He breaketh the bow" (Psalm 46:9). With what result? No arrow can fly through the air to its human target. What is the twentieth-century counterpart? The automatic rifle or machine gun; the fighter plane with its battery of cannon; the submarine with its cargo of deadly nuclear weapons, its powerful torpedoes; the field tank loaded with heavy cannon. Yes, He breaks the bow. All modern weapons are broken by divine judgment.

"He cutteth the spear in sunder" (verse 9). If we take this literally, the javelin in midair is halted in its flight by light— the laser beams of the Almighty, from His fierce arsenal.

Who will doubt that God can intervene and intercept bombs and shells and torpedoes and miraculously preserve the lives of His saints?

"He burneth the chariot in the fire" (verse 9). Here is a picture of a modern battlefield with broken weapons, burned with charred tanks—complete desolation, much like that pictured by the prophet in Isaiah 24:19, 20.

We can see harbingers of such desolation in the havoc wrought by Hurricane Andrew in Homestead, Florida; Hurricane Iniki on the island of Kauai in Hawaii; and the devastation wrought on the island of Guam.

But God has promised that these disasters shall not come nigh His people. Is it not divine providence that God spared Miami, Florida, that populous city, when the hurricane struck south of that metropolitan area and devastated Homestead? Was it not providential that Iniki, the devastating hurricane, bypassed the city of Honolulu on the island of Oahu and struck a smaller island to the west? Why was not New Orleans devastated by Hurricane Andrew? The tragedy struck west of New Orleans. God is sounding a warning, calling all to observe what He can do in providing a sign of the times. Get ready; soon the great cities of the earth will come under the judgments of God.

In the ninety-first psalm, King David warns us about the "snare of the fowler," that is, the "trapper" (NASB).

There is the threatening and noisome pestilence, the arrow that flies by day, the terror by night, the destruction that wastes at noontime. What was he talking about? We do not know, but if we proceed from the known to the unknown, we may rightly suppose that God will permit the recurrence of dreadful pandemics such as the influenza epidemic that killed twenty million people at the close of World War I. Now there is the AIDS plague, with multitudes infected by the HIV virus, with thousands dead and more thousands dying of this incurable disease. But God promises that His people will be delivered. That is the glory of the ninety-first psalm and forty-sixth psalm. There is peril; dangers threaten; but there is miraculous intervention. God spares His precious saints.

"There is much in the world to make us afraid," said F. W. Cropp, "but there is much more in our faith to make us unafraid."

The ninety-first psalm is aimed at answering the most frequently asked question in all Christian discipleship—Why, O God, all these troubles, if You are leading us? If You are with us, why do we have so many problems and painful trials and why not more miraculous evidence of deliverance and safety?

The problems of trials for the saints are numerous, but David learned he needed correction, he could trust the Lord, and if he would abide in the secret place of prayer and devotions, he was guaranteed that the shadow of Jehovah's presence would shield him from the scorching, burning heat of temptation. Besides, God does not permit trials that are more than we can bear.

When confronted with a serious crisis or apparently insurmountable obstacles, how many choose to flee to a mountain of their own creation for some respite from the ordeal. It might be a theater, a television program, a football game, a risqué nightclub, a drinking party—you name it, there are many mountains. But David encourages us. Instead of ducking the problem, face it. Drop down on your knees, and enter the secret place of the Almighty. Before you even know it, the shadow of the all-wise and caring God creeps over you, and you find peace—and a solution—and the power and wisdom to face up to the challenge.

God is there to help fight our battles; to provide forgiveness from the guilt and the power of sin; to soothe our feverish haste and smooth out our brows; to heal our wounds; to assuage our fears and to assure us triumph at last in the struggle against the world, the flesh, and the devil. Think of it!

And think also of the biblical narrative in light of this principle of trusting and depending on God and His precepts of living:

1. Enoch trusted God, and the Lord delivered him bodily from the presence of evil on this disturbed planet.

2. Elijah trusted God, and the Lord carried him away to heaven in a fiery chariot.

3. Moses trusted God, who anointed this senior citizen with power and wisdom, and Moses led Israel from Egypt. At last, he broke forth in resurrection life to follow Enoch and Elijah to the peace of heaven.

4. Job trusted God, though beset by many calamities. His faith faltered but never failed. His faith rewarded him with a larger family, larger herds, and larger faith than he had before.

5. David trusted God through thick and thin. He waited on the Lord's providence, and he landed safely at last on the throne of Israel.

6. Abraham trusted God, obeyed His word, and there on Mount Moriah "sacrificed" his son to God—in spirit, at least—until the voice from heaven stayed his hand, saying, "Lay not thine hand upon the lad, neither do thou any thing unto him: for now I know that thou fearest God, seeing thou hast not withheld thy son, thine only son from me" (Genesis 22:12). Abraham trusted God and His word, obeyed the Lord, and became the father of the faithful.

7. Jesus, during His earthly pilgrimage, relied wholly upon the Father; and when Satan attacked Him, Jesus quoted Psalm

91. The will of God was paramount. "I do always those things that please him," He testified (John 8:29). He abode under the shadow of the Almighty. That was even so in the moment when He said, "My God, my God, why hast thou forsaken me?" (Matthew 27:46). He spoke to God in the secret place of darkness and of thunder.

Hebrews, chapter 11, that great Westminster Abbey of the New Testament, contains the record of heroes and heroines tested by the Lord and proven to be trusting disciples. All of them came from a low place to a high place. They will all be crowned with immortality and will live to testify some day that God's ways are right and just; that God is more than strong enough to lean on! "Whoso is wise, and will observe these things, even they shall understand the lovingkindness of the Lord" (Psalm 107:43). Shall we not live to "sing the song of Moses the servant of God, and the song of the Lamb, saying, Great and marvelous are thy works, Lord God Almighty; just and true are thy ways, thou King of saints. Who shall not fear thee, O Lord, and glorify thy name? for thou only art holy: for all nations shall come and worship before thee; for thy judgments are made manifest" (Revelation 15:3, 4)?

What is it that David had affirmed that called forth God's approval?

He had set his love upon God, as he said in another psalm. "I have set the Lord always before me: because he is at my right hand, I shall not be moved" (Psalm 16:8).

The secret place, the hiding place (see Psalm 32:7), this is the place of prayer, where we call upon the Lord. Here we set our love upon Him, commune with Him by faith, look to Him for help, and receive pardon for sin and the covering of righteousness. Here, too, we are filled with the Holy Spirit, and God changes us, transforming us, making us confident that all is well, since He is in charge, and that we may safely proceed, knowing that He is with us.